<u>Books Elaine has written</u>

1. God's Lent Child, Published by Rose Dog Books.
2. From Baghdad to Suna Migori, Published by Lighthouse Books.
3. Don't Take, Care Take Risks, Published by Austin Macauley.
4. The Mystery of Operation Alphabet, Published by Austin Macauley.

In Memory of:-

In Memory of he people involved with the rescue of 10,000 Jewish Children 1938 – 1939 with the Kindertransport project.

Alfred Batzdorf's Grandmother Martha Ollendorf a member of the 'Jewish Women's League' who helped Alfred and other children escape Nazi Germany.

Sir Nicholas Winton, Trevor Chadwick and Geoff Phelps who brought back children from Prague.

Florence Nankivell who was behind the first Kindertransport from Berlin to UK in December 1938, with the help of Irma Zanker, Max Plaut, Irma Missauer, Dora Magnus, Rafael Plaut, Marie Picard, Dr E Lyon, and Mr Valk.

Erica Gutman, who was behind Jewish children who from Vienna.

Also Beatrice Wellington, Doreen Warriner, the Quakers etc.

In Memory of People from Swanage and Bournemouth, who helped Kinder children 1938-42.

Trevor Chadwick, Rev R.M Chadwick & Chadwick Family, Mr Geoff Phelps & Phelps family. Smedmore Towers School in Kimmeridge. (Near Corfe Castle.) Bournemouth Refugee Committee Mr Jackson, Miss Madeline West and Simon (her friend.) Reverend F. S. Horan, Rabbi Helipern, Mrs Cohen, Hills – Brown family, Gilpin – Browns family. The American family Elkington's, Captain Patterson, Dr Woodroffe, Tony Crawshaw, Mr Davies, Dr Risk, Mr and Mrs Hawes and their family. Doreen Sears, the Talbot family & Isabelle Wilson. Elaine Heggie and Mrs T.W. Style. Mr Legchalles, Mr Spurrel and Ethel Anne Mooring Aldridge.

Kindertransport Children

From Prague Peter Walder, Willy Weigl, Marietta Wolf-Ferrari. (Phelps) Hannah Stern, Gerda Stein, (Mayer)

From Berlin Kindertransport Alfred Batzdorf via Bournemouth Refugee Committee. Other children who came through Bournemouth Refugee Committee were Kurt Eisenbach, Edward Merkel, Millie Loewenstein, Virgil and Friedl Berger. Lotte and Herbert Wolff and a third Kindertransport child who survived the war, but later was killed on a ship taking passengers to Canada. Gary Saul Berlin Kinder Transport. Children who are unknown to me brought to Swanage through these agencies.

In Memory

10,000 children rescued by the Kindertransport project.
1.5 Million Jewish children alone who were murdered by the Nazi Regime.

IN MEMORY OF THE LATE ALFRED BATZDORF
1922-2022

Genesis 12 v 1-3

"Get out of your country,
From your family
And from your father's house,
To a land that I will show you.
2 I will make you a Great Nation;
I will bless you
And make your name great;
And you shall be a blessing.
3 I will bless those who bless you,
And I will curse him who curses you; (despise you in Hebrew)
And in you all the families of the earth shall be blessed."

Promise and Covenant to Abraham by God.

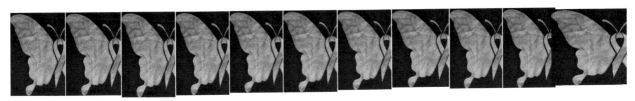

THE BUTTERFLY

The reason why I chose this collage for the front page of my book, which I created at the 'Art Workshop' in 'All Saints Church', Swanage, is because it shows what the Kindertransport children who came to UK were saved from. These children were spared from being amongst the 1.5 million Jewish children who were murdered or died in the concentration camps and ghettos during the Holocaust. Thousands of children especially twins were used in medical experiments, others were gassed in vans and in gas chambers. Some were starved, and others died in terrible conditions in the ghettos and in the concentration camps.

Therefore at the top of the picture we have a very tatty butterfly next to children in the ghetto where there were no butterflies. At the bottom of the picture there are a few beautiful butterflies representing the children who escaped the Nazis Regime via Kindertransport. Some of the Kinder children came to Swanage where there were hundreds of butterflies flying around naturally. I chose butterflies also because of a poignant poem called 'The Butterfly' by Pavel Friedman.

The Butterfly
By Pavel Friedman
The last,the very last,
So richly, brightly, dazzling yellow
Is carried way up high.
It went away I'm sure because
It wished to kiss the world goodbye.
For seven weeks I've lived in here
Pinned up inside the ghetto
But I have found what I love here.
The dandelions call to me
And the white Chestnut branches in the court.
Only I never saw another butterfly
That butterfly was the last one
Butterflies don't live here in the ghetto.

Elaine Merrikin Trimlett Glover

Swanage
Kindertransport
And The
Bournemouth Refugee Committee
Connection.

A CIP catalogue record for this title is available from the British library

ISBN ISBN is 978-1-3999-7734-0

UK ISBN & SAN Agencies
Nielsen Book Services Limited
Tel +44 (0)1483 712215 Fax +44 (0)1483 712214

Second Edition 07/05/2024

Introduction

In the 1930's in the wake of the Nazi regime orchestrating anti-Semitic violence including Kristallnacht (the night of the broken glass) where Jewish businesses, shops were ransacked, and windows smashed, Jewish Synagogues, and orphanages burned down, and many Jews were arrested, and sent to 'Birkenau Concentration Camp,' and the Government began to take notice of what was happening, and how serious this was becoming to the Jewish Community.

On the 25th November 1938, five days after Kristallnacht a delegation of British Jews, and leaders from the Quakers went to see Prime Minister Neville Chamberlin in the House of Commons where they debated the growing refugee crisis n Europe which led to what was called Kindertransport. (Children's transport from Germany to UK and other countries). This came about when the leaders of these groups requested that the British Government permitted the temporary admission of unaccompanied Jewish children, without their parents.

The British Cabinet debated these issues the following day and subsequently prepared a bill to present to Parliament and they passed a bill which stated that the government would waive certain immigration requirements so as to allow the entry into Great Britain of unaccompanied children ranging from infants up to the age of seventeen, under a number of conditions. Sir Samuel Hoare agreed to speed up the immigration process by allowing travel documents to be issued on a group basis rather than individually that no limit was placed on the number of refugees was publicly announced.

The Colonial Office turned down the Jewish agencies' separate request to allow the admission of 10,000 children to British-controlled manadotory Palastine. The Palastinian Jewish agencies then increased their planned target number to 15,000 unaccompanied children to enter Great Britain in this way

During the morning of 21st November 1938, the Home Secretary Sir Samuel Hoare, Home Secretary and met a large delegation representing Jewish groups, as well as Quaker and other non-Jewish groups, working on behalf of refugees. The groups, though considering all refugees, were specifically allied under a non-denominational organisation called the "Movement for the Care of Children" from Germany. This organisation was considering only the rescue of children, who would need to leave their parents behind in Germany.

In that debate of 21ˢᵗ November 1938, Sir Samuel Hoare paid particular attention to the plight of children. Very importantly, he reported that enquiries in Germany had determined that, most remarkably, nearly every parent asked had said that they would be willing to send their child off unaccompanied to the United Kingdom, leaving their parents behind.

Although Sir Samuel Hoare declared that he and the Home Office "shall put no obstacle in the way of children coming here," the agencies involved had to find homes for the children and also fund the operation to ensure that none of the refugees would become a financial burden on the public. Every child had to have a guarantee of £50 to finance his or her eventual re-emigration, as it was expected the children would stay in the country only temporarily. Hoare made it clear that the monetary and housing and other aid required had been promised by the Jewish community and other communities.

Kindertransport was a unique humanitarian rescue programme which ran between November 1938, to September 1939 and they were led by a number of very courageous people who put their own lives on the line to save approximately 10.000 mainly Jewish children or children whose parents were associated with anti-Nazi political groups or who didn't fit in with Nazi Germany Arian Race.

These people were the like of Florence Nankivell, who led the very first Kindertransport December 1ˢᵗ-2ⁿᵈ 1938 from Berlin to UK,Trevor Chadwick and Sir Nicholas Winton who ran the Kindertransport from Prague to UK. In December 1938, Mrs Gertruida Mijsmullar Mcijer a Dutch freedom fighter, led a unique humanitarian rescue programme between November 1938-1939, with a number of mainly Jewish Kindertransport children to Holland. In December 1938, Doreen Warriner laid unknowingly the foundations of the Kindertransport with her voluntary work helping adult refugees escape from Czechoslovakia, which earned her an OBE.

These very courageous people who laid their own lives down to rescue the vulnerable children who lived in dangerous times when they had no future but the death camps. Irma Zanker when on the return from of one of her trips to UK with the Kindertransport children, she herself was arrested, and sent to Theresienstadt and then Auschwitz where she perished.

One of the places were some children were sent to for a short while was the sea side resort of Swanage on the Jurassic Coast line, care of Florence Nankivell and Bournemouth / Swanage Refugee Committee, plus Trevor Chadwick / Sir Nicholas Winton. People who served on the Bournemouth Refugee Committee according to the account of Alfred Batzdorf was Miss West and her friend Simon (unknown surname), Mr Phil Carter, Dr Woodroffe, Captain Paterson, the Gilpin- Browns, the Hill-Browns, Mrs Cohn, Rabbi Helipern, a pottery shop owner, Rev and Mrs Horan.

Table of Contents

Chapter 1
What the Kindertransport children were saved from.

Chapter 2
How I got involved with Kindertransport.

Chapter 3
Florence Nankivell
By Edmund Nankivell

Chapter 4
Irma Zanker (My distant Cousin)
Child escort on the very first Kindertransport

Chapter 5
Max Plaut
Child escort on the very first Kindertransport

Chapter 6
Poem 'Leaving Berlin'
by Elaine Merrikin Trimlett Glover

With Thanks.

Chapter 1
What the Kindertransport children were saved from.

The Kindertransport Children were saved from being gassed in concentration camps, and gassed in vans, starvation, disease, and being used for experimentation. Almost 1.5 Million Jewish children were murdered by the Nazi regime in the Holocaust, as well as any other children i.e. 'Gypsy Roma Travellers', and German disabled children, that didn't fall into the category of the Arian race .

Two Jewish children with the 'Star of David.'
Jewish children murdered by the Nazis.

This young lady was murdered by being injected in the heart with Phenyl.

Chapter 2

How I got involved with Kindertransport research.

I have been very interested in my ancestry for a long time, and I knew that we have ancestry from the Zanker family, but I didn't for some reason take much notice of where they came from, and the meaning of the name Zanker until I began to volunteer at a Christian Radio called 'Hope FM.' I had interviewed Lynda Ford - Horne, a Jewish lady from the Bournemouth Reform Synagogue who leads the Holocaust Educational group. She came with Betty, who leads the the 'Roma group' in Bournemouth. During the Holocaust up to 1.5 million of the 'Roma' population were killed by the 'Nazi Regime' in WW2. This is why Betty talks about the Roma Community in Dorset, to help them get support.

I was also invited to the Wimborne Holocaust Memorial, Wimborne Minister, Organised by Edith Powney. We accepted the invitation and took our elderly Aunty Yvonne who at the time was 102 and is now 107. Despite her age she had never heard of, or seen photos of Jewish people who had been starved almost to death in the Nazi Concentration Camps. This is why it was a great eye opener for her and indeed a great shock.

We also met Henry Schachter who had been rescued as a child just at the beginning of the WW2, from the hands of the Nazis. He came and shared his story on my Christian Radio Show in Bournemouth along with two of his friends including Walter Kamerling. Walter was a Kindertransport child sent to Northern Ireland for the duration of the war. It seemed more and more like the pieces of a jigsaw puzzle were coming together as I interviewed a number of people who shared their story about how they were saved from the Holocaust as children.

During my meetings and interviews on the radio I met Dawn Cook whose grandmother lived in Billesdon, Leicestershire and was of Jewish descent. As we spoke for a long time on the phone the name Zanker came to mind. My great, great, great, grandmother Charlotte Zanker whose ancestry went right the way back to 1735, when a Joseph Zanker who was a sojourner (a temporary resident,) arrived in Billesdon and his line produced many generations of Zanker's, of which I am one. Typing Zanker confirmed that the family were of Jewish origin, and may have come from Prussia or Northern Europe. However the most harrowing fact was that there were many Zanker's who were documented as having been murdered in Auschwitz.

Paula Zanker was a lawyer and after the war she went to the Nuremberg trials to represent the Jewish survivors of Vilna Ghetto, to explain how SS Major Plague had saved 100's of Jews from the gas chambers by giving the Jewish people jobs even though they had never trained for that trade before.

Irma Zanker was a school teacher who went on a number of the Kindertransport journeys taking mostly Jewish children from Berlin to UK just before WW2, and sadly she was sent to Theresienstadt, and then Auschwitz where she perished.

Klaus Zanker another of my distant Zanker relatives was only very young when he and his family were sent to the Isle of Man to an Internment Camp after the 'Night of the 'Broken Glass' as his his father Elias had bad mouthed the Nazis. He remembered his father stating that it was more like a holiday camp than and internment camp. Here German's and Jews were interned together as they were all seen as enemies of Britain in WW2. Klaus, and his family were then sent to London where his father became a 'Shoe Smith' and he and his family received a 'Nationalization Certificate'.

Just before lockdown in late 2019, Edith Powney came on Purbeck Coast Radio 'Lunch time with Elaine' where I interviewed her about the guest speakers and guest vocalists at the Holocaust Memorial Wimborne Minster. Obviously my show had to have a Swanage connection and so I googled up Swanage and Holocaust on Google search and it came up with Trevor Chadwick. Trevor was a teacher from Forres School Swanage and he along with his co-worker Sir Nicholas Winton, rescued 669 mostly Jewish Children from Nazis Germany.

I discovered after the night of the 'Broken Glass', in Berlin, people around the world including Britain realised that the Nazis were greatly anti-Semitic and against the Jewish Community. Therefore the British Government realised something needed to be done to help the children escape from Nazis Europe. Various religious groups and those who were sympathetic to Jewish children, began the process of bringing these children to UK via the Kindertransport with people like Trevor Chadwick, Sir Nicholas Winton and Florence Nankivell.

After the radio show, I did quite a lot of research and found Trevor's niece Annie Bridger, who lives in Swanage when I found her brother Toby on Facebook. I also discovered Edmund Nankivell the son of Florence Nankivell. Edmund told me that his mother was behind the very first Kindertransport from Berlin to UK in 1938, the same Kindertransport Alfred Batzdorf came on to Swanage from Berlin.

Annie, and I met up in Swanage to discuss Trevor and we both thought there should be a memorial for Trevor somewhere in Swanage and we came up with the idea of a statue. Annie already had an idea who should sculpt it and we met with local sculptor Moira Purver, in a Swanage a Cafe to discuss this. Moira was very keen to sculpt the statue of Trevor and she had read many books about Trevor Chadwick to get an idea of his character. Annie and I later went to a 'Swanage Town Council' meeting where we put out the idea of having a statue of Trevor Chadwick somewhere in Swanage. Annie's cousin Jonathon and his wife also attended the meeting give Annie family support.

Whist there I gave a short talk about the importance of Trevor Chadwick and Nicholas Winton's project saving 669 Jewish children's lives and I shared about what happened to the Jewish children in the consecration camps. All in all the Town Council took everything we had said on board. They also listened to Councillor Bill Trite, who had also been researching Trevor Chadwick at the same time as myself. The Town council agreed to the proposal of the statue and that Moira was to sculpt it.

From this Town Council meeting, the 'Trevor Chadwick Memorial Trust' came in to being which consisted of retired Magistrate and Estate Agent John Corbin, ex mayor Mike Bonfield, retired Magistrate Josephine Jackson who works with 'Holocaust Education' sharing about Kindertransport and also a member of the Jewish Hebrew Synagogue. Councillor Bill Trite, ex mayor Avril Harris, Annie Bridger representing the Trevor Chadwick family, plus other councillors and members of the Swanage community .

In 2022 the Statue was unveiled by Samuel Chadwick, Trevor's grandson and also Sir Nicholas Winton's son, Nick Winton, which was both very poignant and meaningful. Sadly, Nick's sister Barbara Winton who I'd interviewed on radio on a number of occasions,was too ill to travel and shortly afterwards, she sadly passed away. Had Barbara have been well I know she would have attended the unveiling of Trevor's statute.

Amongst the supporters of the unveiling of the 'Trevor Chadwick Statute' were Trevor's family and the Trevor Chadwick Trust, Rabbi Jesner and Michaels from the Jewish community and a member from AJR, (Association of Jewish Refugees), myself and members of Purbeck Coast Radio, plus many people connected with Kindertransport.

This is why I wanted to write 'Swanage And The Kindertransport, Bournemouth Refugee Committee Connection,' in honour of the Swanage community both past and present as its been a very significant seaside town. They reached out to the Kindertransport supporting the refugees as Swanage community still reaches out to the community today with various groups, including those connected to the local church.

Recently Swanage community provided two boxes of nail polish to give to 'Church on the Streets' in Burnley, where the Pastor's wife has a ministry helping the homeless by polishing their nails. She also chats to the women who are, or who have been homeless with different social needs. 'Church on the Streets' had been visited by Prince and Princess of Wales William and Kate, who like me were very touched by their ministry and all they do to support their very poor community.

Chapter 3
Florence Nankivell

FLORENCE 1950

By Edmund Nankivell.

"Florence Nankivell my mother was the 'mastermind' behind the very first 'Kindertransport' which took Jewish Children from Berlin, centre of Nazi Germany, to the Hook of Holland, and then to safety in the UK December 1st - 2nd 1938. All Jewish children were accepted, however adults could only if they had employment in the UK or were married to a British citizen. This is why foster families were needed and found. In order to understand my mother's intention one has to look back in her past.

Amsterdam
In the 1920's Florence, single and aged 22, was already involved in charitable work with the M.A.I Bureau in Amsterdam.

Trinidad
Florence married in 1932 and lived in Trinidad where her husband (my father) was posted in the Government Office as Deputy Colonial Secretary. Whilst she was in Trinidad, she had noticed great poverty: local children did not go to school or if they did they could not pay full attention to the teacher because they were hungry - these children were from poor families and were not given any breakfast. So my mother Florence set up a charity called "the Children of the Breakfast Sheds" which was very successful and helped the local children to have a good breakfast and be able to concentrate on their lessons.

UK - December 1938
So it is no surprise that when Florence was back in UK in 1938 she was keen to help in some ways and continue with charitable work.

December 1st-2nd 1938.
Florence helped organise the very first train of Jewish children to safety from Berlin to the Hook of Holland and then to UK. In Berlin on her way to collect the Jewish children she was hassled by the Nazi Police, why a Protestant priest who was with

Florence deserted her before the train entered Berlin, leaving her on her own. Nevertheless, with full courage and determination, Florence collected the Jewish children in Berlin and travelled by train with them through the Netherlands to the sea port Hook of Holland, then crossing to Harwich in UK before reaching London where foster families were waiting. Florence was prepared to do a second Kindertransport trip but her handlers advised her against it as she had been hassled by the Gestapo while in Berlin and it was considered unsafe. My mother Florence did many other admirable things in her life but Kindertransport is the one I am most proud of. There is a book about my father's work in Trinidad where Florence is also mentioned. The book is called "The Price of Conscience" by Brinsley Samaroo."

(Alfred Batzdorf to whom the book is dedicated to was on Florence Nankivell's Kindertransport and he was sent to Swanage by the Bournemouth Refugee Committee.)

This is a document which shows the names of the teachers who were sent to escort the children on the very first Kindertransport, 'masterminded' by Florence Nankivell.

Chapter 4
Irma Zanker

Irma Zanker a distant relative, was a special needs teacher and her job title was "Work Educator in the Hamburg Workshops for the Disabled." Irma Zanker was a native of Hamburg and born in Altona. Irma was divorced and became a single parent to her to her son called 'Klaus Peter Juergen Zanker'. The very year Hitler came to power Irma was sacked from the 'Hamburger Werkstätten' in 1933, and then worked as a stenographer and typist with the Jewish community.

The night of the broken glass 'Kristallnacht' where Jewish homes, Synagogues, and orphanges were burned to the ground, as were shops, and businesss by the Nazis. This meant that Jewish Communities were in great danger as they were under attack and faced extreme antisemitismn. One of the main responses from the British Governement and various religious and humanitarian groups, was to bring Jewish children to the UK with the Kinderstranport Project. Irma herself travelled as an escort for the Kindertransport children on a couple of occasions to the UK, escorting mostly Jewish refugees. On her very first trip to UK she escorted, Alfred Baztdorf, who was sent to Swanage, Dorset, December 1st -2nd 1938. Alfred's guarantor was the Bournemouth Refugee Committee who paid the £50 guarantee. On another occassion Irma escorted more children to UK on January 17th 1939, on board the S.S. Manhattan to UK. Time was of the essence to get as many mostly Jewish children out of Nazi Germany as soon as possible.

On Irma's return she moved to 'Judenhaus' (Jewish house) with her sister Fanny David, her mother and son Klaus. Irma was later questioned by the Gestapo where she mentioned that she intended to emigrate to England. However Irma Zanker's plan failed as she was arrested and sent to Terezin and was later murdered in Auschwitz. A stumbling stone (stolperstein) lies in front of her house today.

However Klaus, Irma's son escaped to England through the Kindertransport project two months later. According to German researchers, Klaus fled first to London and then he moved to Scotland where he later changed his name to Peter David, Gordon-Sinclair and whilst living in Finchley, North London he was naturalised as British in 1947. In 1948 he married Jean Esther Gordon in Glasgow and according to the census in 1962 they lived at 9 Fotheringay Road, Glasgow and in1978 he remarried a second wife Rose Levenson. I remember a few years ago that someone was trying to make contact with Irma's son Klaus but got him mixed up with another relative of mine also called Klaus but Unfortunately Klaus wasn't the person that the researcher was looking for. Klaus my other relative was a child at beginning of WW2 and spent a short time in the Isle of Man detention centre with his family and then later they were sent to London after they left the detention centre and his parents were naturalised in UK and his father worked as a shoe maker.

Chapter 5
Max Plaut
An escort on the very first Kindertransport from Berlin to UK
(Taken from 'Lior Oran technology & history Hamburg to Tel -Aviv')

Max Plaut, born in 1901 the son of of a teacher, was the Chairman of the Hamburg Jewish Community, escorted children along with Irma Zanker and a number of other people on the very first Kindertransport from Berlin to UK December 1st - 2nd 1938, through Florence Nankivell. Max was seriously injured in WW1, and then he became a banker and a member of the Freemasons. Max was an anti-Zionist, the founder of the anti-Zionist Jewish Youth in Germany, and German Nationalist. He was defined as 'German by culture, but was Jewish by religion and origin.'

The essence of Max's role in those impossible times, was to ensure the safety and well-being of the Jews (including financial management of the community, raising money outside of Germany to help Jews with emigration) and at the same time to fulfil, transfer and execute the orders of the Nazi Government, through the Gestapo. He wasn't the only leader of the Hamburg community who managed and led the community's life: but also Leo Lippmann, Joseph Carlebach, and Max Warburg who owned the Warburg Bank.

Each did whatever they could and hoped to do and that with careful planning, and navigation of the ship, they could help take the community through the storm of those days. Max had an excellent diplomatic talent and an even better sense of humour. With the help of those qualities, he stayed in a positive, though not an equal, relationship with the Gestapo Officers, and mainly with the Hamburg Police Chief in charge of Jewish affairs. The Police Chief was called Klaus Gottche and they respected each other. He often used manipulations, without fear, with great courage, with black humour, and great audacity. It didn't always help him, and Plaut was arrested, and even beaten a few times by Gottche's subordinates:

For example, in 1938, many Jews from the community were arrested and Plaut was among them. He was held in a cell for a day and a half with no food and water. Since he didn't want to die like that, he called the guard. The guard asked him why does he dare to call him, and noted that 1200 Jews were sent to camps from that same prison.
 Max rudely asked: "So what happens now?"
-"I will go to check" answered the guard.
    Not long after Max was released from his cell and transferred to his "friend" Gottche's office. Gottche scolds him "where have you been? We've been looking for you."

-"You're supposed to know, you picked me up from the cell." said Plaut.
-"I don't know what to do with you."said Gottche.
-"you better think about it while I'm waiting at my house" Plaut answered him rudely, and so it was. He was sent to his house and was obligated to report to the police station twice a day.

Max's connections with the Gestapo created serious unjust allegations towards Plaut after the war, of collaborating with the Nazis – It is now possible to understand that Max didn't actually 'collaborate', but he did follow orders. He made lists of Jews, but not agreeing to do that wouldn't have stopped the Nazi plan, at least by acting, he softened the blow until the last moment and sometimes he even saved Jews, as will be described later.

The immigration of the Jews – Organization
After the Pogrom Night 'Kristallnacht' while many Jews were arrested and shipped to camps all over the Reich, Max was able to free and rescue most of Hamburg's Jews with negotiations, and got them visas and money to emigrate, mostly to South American States.

After the visas to 'South American States ' started to end, Max began, to 'fake and forge visas' to those countries with the help of the Gestapo. The Nazis used the forced escape of the Jews to bring in foreign money to the country: a Jew could only leave if he paid in foreign money, which helped the economy greatly, and imprisoned those who had money but couldn't get foreign money. The family of the person writing these lines, was a wealthy family from Hamburg, and they couldn't leave the country because the money needed for it was asked from Max's grandmother in Palestine. She didn't have it as an emigrant and that's how they found their death at the camps. The Nazis did everything to make the Jews leave. The law didn't interest them and they mostly ignored border rules when someone without a visa left.

Adolf Eichmann's Travel Agency
Adolf Eichmann went even further and established the 'Travel Agency' of the Reich to coordinate and hold the cruise line from Germany to Palestine, even during the war when the borders were closed.

After a while and after saving many Jews, the German shipping company accused him of its entanglements overseas due to illegal passengers. He was tried in Germany, but the main Gestapo headquarters in Berlin asked for the charges against him to be dropped.

As a result, he was asked by the headquarters in Berlin to stop forging visas and Plaut told them that this is the only way to save Jews from the camps and everything was done with the approval of the Gestapo headquarters in Hamburg.

The war

The beginning of the war was confusing for Plaut and the Jews. A number of months earlier, in a speech he gave, Hitler promised that the Jews will suffer if a war will be "forced" on Germany. Also, his ties inside the SS told him, "If there will be a war, the Jews will be the first to lose and initially, the older Jews will be taken to forced labour camps".

Max Plaut in a testimonial from the Eichmann Nuremberg trial:

"June 1939 I came back to Germany from London. I was in the main office of the Gestapo in Hamburg. I was questioned by the Jewish department because I came from abroad. There was a war psychosis and the topic came up immediately and the man said, that if there would be a war the Jews would be the first to lose. "you'll see miracles and wonders" he said. ...and what happened in November 1938 is a dress rehearsal only." The Gestapo officials and the Nazi party every time they had good news they said they were thinking about making detention and concentration camp for all the Jews."

Chapter 6

Leaving Berlin December 1ˢᵗ 1938

"By Elaine Merrikin Trimlett Glover 2023 "

Why am I on this train leaving Berlin
Why am I waving mama and papa goodbye
Why do they have strange smiles on their faces
Not happy but smiles of desperation
Tears streaming down my parents faces.

All I have is a little brown leather suitcase with a pair of trousers,
Shirt, socks, pants and my teddy bear.
Where am I going
Why are all these children on this train
All with one leather suitcase
Some had a doll
Some had a toy
Some with no toys at all to cling on to
For some sort of comfort
To muffle anxieties and fear.

The sound of Nazis boots marching down the corridor
Everyone sitting in fear of 'what's next'
Little girl next to me starts to cry
So I hold her hand and put my finger to my mouth
To hopefully let her know to
Shhhhh,
Nazi soldier walks past and we keep our heads down.

I don't want to leave mama, papa and grandmother
I don't want to leave my friends and my family
I don't want to leave my doggy, I love my doggy.
A lady escorting us to England
walks past counting every child.
The boy across from me
Was put on the train
Then taken off by his Mama in tears hugging him
Like she'd never hugged her son before
Then she put him back on the train in a moment of desperation.
After the realization he couldn't stay in Berlin.
Now he clings onto his tin plane in his pocket.

The train stops and we are now in Holland
Some elderly ladies get on the train with welcoming hot chocolate drinks
As we wait to get off and get on a ship to England.
Across the sea far far far away
Who'd have thought ?

The Nazis no longer walk up and down the corridor
A sigh of relief that desperation of the unknown has subsided.
The Lady escorting us beckons us to leave the train in an orderly fashion
I wake up the little girl next to me as she sleeps
Her doll clenched to her chest.

The ladies who joined the train came on the boat
Giving us more tea and chocolate
More loving kindness
Then as fast as they came they were gone.
But where were we going to ?
Where were we going to stay ?
Why had we been taken from our parents ?
Why had they abandoned us ?
What was going to happen to them ?
More and more questions filled my head.
More fears, new fears, new questions.

I got off the train holding the little girls hand
She drops the doll onto the train line.
Crossing the train track to get to the Station
Little girl begins to want to run.
Holding her hand tightly I dragged her along
Whispering in her ear 'Leave the doll behind,'shh
Two by two we marched towards the ship
You could smell the ships steam and coal burning in the night air.
I am no longer a little boy
But a young man
Awaiting what fate lies ahead...

We all clambered on to the boat, and sat down again exhausted
The journey seemed endless.
The journey seemed never ending
Lying on a bunk bed
You could feel the boat toss around in the sea
Moving up and down, up and down.
Children being sick
Groaning, wrenching, when will this stop ?
Will this journey ever end ?

Suddenly we were told to line up to disembark the boat
Exhausted children
Stood still and were silent
Numb, weak and tired
Suddenly the thought came to me
We had landed in heaven
No Nazis, no discrimination,
No fear of being taken to Bergen Belson
Expectations, excitement,
began to bubble up within us and outwards.

Now we were off the boat
At last!
Onto another train
But this time we are heading to the 'New Jerusalem'
Dovercourt where we would be checked for fleas, ill health
Handed over to someone who would pay the £50 guarantee
Then onwards and upwards to a place called Swanage.

Chapter 7
Holocaust Memorial Wimborne Minster,
By Edith Powney

(Golden Minora dish, by Elaine Merrikin Trimlett Glover, made in Swanage Art Club.)

"Speaking to men in a prison some years ago, Alec Ward (Abram Warsaw, 1929 – 2018) said he knew what it was like to be imprisoned. He had been in two ghettos, three slave labour camps and two concentration camps.
'My only crime' he told them, was that 'I was a Jew'.
When the camp was liberated, Alec was found skeletal and naked alongside other Jews in Mauthausen.

Holocaust Memorial is a time to remember the six million Jews, of whom one and a half million Jews were children, all murdered in the Nazi attempt to do away with the Jewish people in Europe. However, we cannot detach ourselves from the long history of anti-Semitism in England. Violent attacks against Jews took place at the end of the 12th century and in 1218 Jews were forced to wear a distinguishing badge, an order later revived by Hitler. The expulsion of the Jews from England came by royal decree in 1290 and it was not until 400 years later that Jewish people were permitted to settle in this country. The word 'ghetto' was the Italian word for the building in medieval Venice where Jewish people in Italy were once enclosed. The Spanish Inquisition epitomised the cruelty meted out to the Jewish people. Persecution in Europe drove Jews further east and many settled in in Russia, but 'Fiddler on the Roof' tells of the pogroms that Jewish people faced there at the end of the 19th century. In 2017, the first Holocaust Memorial was held in Wimborne Minster when the focus was the suffering of children in the Terezin, the ghetto near

Prague, as it was recalled in the music of the 'Oratorio Terezin' and the film 'I Will Not Die'. 15,000 children went through that camp and fewer than 100 survived.

In 2018, Henry Schachter told how as a child he was hidden by a family in Belgium spending most of those years, for safety, in the basement of their house. The story of Regine Miller who was also hidden in Belgium was heard too. The title of the book she wrote is 'Tell No One Who You Are'.

Erica Prean, who died on 23 December 2022, spoke in 2019 of the fear she remembers growing up in Aachen in the days leading up to Kristallnacht and John Fieldsend recalled his boyhood in Dresden and his escape from Czechoslovakia on the Kindertransport. His book is called 'A Wondering Jew'.

A video was shown of Felicia Carmelly, who died in 2019, speaking about the 'killing fields of Transnistria', the deportation and killing of Jewish people in eastern Romania driven across the Dniester River, as she wrote in her book 'Across the rivers of memory, published by the Azrieli Foundation.

In 2020, a video of 'Fountain of Tears' was screened and the message given was a call to repentance for the anti-Semitism that lingers on in church and nation. In 1945 the British government offered to take in 1000 young Jewish people who had survived the Holocaust. Only 732 could be found. Some of their stories, including the reminiscences of Alec Ward, are recorded in 'The Boys' a book by the historian Sir Martin Gilbert. The Service held in Wimborne Minster in 2023 focused on the children who perished in the Holocaust and on the suffering of those like Alec Ward whose story was told by his grandson, Liron Velleman.

Jane Moxon spoke of the thousands of Jewish children in France who were sent to Auschwitz but also how many children were hidden in the homes of French people who risked their lives in saving these young Jewish lives from death.

There was a return to the history of Terezin (Theresienstadt as it was called by the Nazis) through a video showing the closing scenes of the opera 'Brundibar', by Hans Krasa, performed in 1944 by children, nearly all of whom were sent to the gas chambers.

Local school children read poems written by Jewish children in Terezin. This ghetto in Czechoslovakia was created to cover up the Nazi genocide of the Jews. With its high proportion of artists, musicians and intellectuals, culture flourished in the ghetto – alongside starvation, disease and the constant dread of transports to the east. Videos from the Children's Memorial at Yad Vashem were shown at the beginning of the 2023 remembrance of the Holocaust in Wimborne Minster.

Names of the children who perished in the Shoah, (Hebrew for catastrophe,) can be heard at the Yad Vashem, the World Holocaust Remembrance Centre in Jerusalem. The name Yad Vashem, taken from Isaiah 56:5 means 'a memorial and a name.' It takes three months for the names and dates of birth and death of all who perished, to be recited. We are reminded of the life of which each child was robbed, the anguish of families and the loss to our world of the gifts and contributions that each could have made to the world they were so cruelly taken from. We remember the Holocaust survivors today, for whom the pain of the memory of the families lost to them never goes away.

Children saved by the Kindertransport were also remembered and the statue to Trevor Chadwick in nearby Swanage, a long over-due tribute to a man who saved so many mostly Jewish children from the jaws of death at the hands of the Nazis. Ralph Goldenberg recalled this history and called us to remember *(zakar)* in Hebrew, to keep the memory alive of the six million Jewish men, women and children murdered in the Holocaust.

Six candles were lit in silence by Holocaust survivor, Henry Schachter, Tony Horitz and Abraham Bossem, who both lost family members in the Shoah, Alistair Scott from the Joseph Storehouse Trust, artist Wendy Foot and Alison Eastwood from Ebenezer Operation Exodus.

Verses from the Hebrew scriptures were sung by Alex Cook, accompanied by pianist, Cynthia Wilson. Violinist Emma-Marie Kabanova played 'My Heart within me is desolate' (Psalm 143:4) music composed by Judith Lang Zimont. After the lighting of the candles Emma-Marie played music from Schindler's List and people left to the sound of the violin playing a Yiddish folksong 'Oyfn Pripetshik'.The service closed with a video of the Aaronic blessing sung in Hebrew by artist 'Joshua Aaron' in Jerusalem.

May the remembrance of the Holocaust be not forgotten and the words spoken to Abram **'I will bless those who bless you and curse those who despise you and in you all the families of the earth will be blessed' (Genesis 12:3)."**

By
Edith Powney.

Chapter 8

By Alfred Batzdorf

1922 - 2022 aged 100.

He was a Kindertransport child who was sent to Swanage on the very first
Kindertransport from Berlin to UK December 1 – 2nd 1938.
Alfred also shared these memoirs on a video with Holocaust Memorial Oral History
(https://collections.ushmm.org/search/catalog/irn509536)

Anne and Michael Filer shared an article written by Alfred which says ;-
   "When we talk of the Kindertransport we talk of one event in our history, yet this
event concerned 10,000 children, so it is important to realise that on a personal level
it really consists of thousands of different stories.

   First of all it concerns individuals, and no two of them are alike, people yes
even kids differ in their reaction to events which are thrust upon them, Those
children spanned different age groups from two to seventeen, and surely their
experiences were not the same; they came from different family backgrounds and
the experience of separation from their parents wouldn't have affected each child in
the same way. Also, and probably most importantly, the way each child was
accommodated in England differed widely.

   Some were taken into families as a 'mothers help', some were considered as the
same level as their own children; some were placed into hostels, some in private
homes and some others were taken in as foster children against payment by one of
the relief agencies. So you see my story may have been totally different from the
other children.

I was on the very first Kindertransport which arrived in England on December 1st - 2nd 1938, just barely after 'kristallnacht' which gave the impetus for the entire rescue operation, (As a footnote to the story, it is very interesting to note that it only took three weeks to introduce a bill in the Commons debate it, pass it into the law build up the necessary infrastructure, on both sides of the channel, until the first child arrived in England,)

Yes I was on the Kindertransport, I was one of eldest ones and how did it come about? It all started with 'Kristallnacht', I was arrested by the Gestapo, though I was only 16 years old, for the simple reason my father wasn't at home, so they took me. The next day, when all the men were taken to 'Buchenwald Konzentratoinslager', I absented myself from the group. I was an escapee, and had to get out of the country, thus there was no separation trauma, my separation from my parents was seen by us all as my only chance of survival and even theirs.

My grandmother who lived in Berlin was Martha Ollendorf and she was in the active 'Jewish Women's League' a group responsible for preparing the collective passport lists. Since I couldn't obtain a passport by other means, I was able to have my name added to their list. Martha Ollendorf was later sent to Theresienstadt concentration camp where she was murdered by the 'Nazi Regime.'

I could absolutely remember nothing of my departure from Breslau, the town where we all lived. I faintly remember my grandmother having taken me to the railway station in Berlin, but at best very sketchily, it certainly leave the impact a traumatic experience would have had. In fact the most bits of my memory consist of the dreaded customs inspections.

It turned out as most contacts with German authorities at the time, rather uniformly. Some were very business like and some what cursory, others more violent getting their kicks by harassing people, like turning some kids suitcases upside down. Yet, I distinctly remember when we crossed the border and everyone, and that is everyone
who was old enough to understand the significance, breathed a big sigh of relief! Then I remember the English Channel, which was a pretty stormy time of the year and the sea was quite violent causing the fellow in the bunk bellow me to be be violently sick, constantly moaning he was puking his gallbladder out."

Alfred also wrote an essay about his early life and he writes "This section is the edited version of an essay which was written only a few years after my arrival in the US. It contains material which I could not have recalled today, but which must be authentic since they were recorded so shortly after their occurrence."

The Next Two Years -England

1.How they cared for us

"Those channel ships had a tough time ploughing there way across the water from the continent to the British Isles during the rough winter months. I was on one of them together with hundreds of Jewish children during the night of December 1st-2nd 1938, breathing free as we were approaching a haven of safety, yet deeply concerned for our dear ones who stayed behind in the country of concentration camps, of 'infamy' and 'bigotry.'

When dawn arrived we went topside. The sea was calm now as we were cruising up the East Coast of England, the outline of the coast was barely visible off the port side. There were buses waiting for us when we disembarked at Harwich. A short ride through the snappy morning air brought us to a camp, 'Dovercourt Bay Holiday Lido.' The camp, ordinarily closed during the winter months, was made available to an organization taking care of refugee children.

I spent a couple of weeks there where we were housed in single bedrooms accessible from the walk, in front of one storey buildings which were summer houses

for vacationing kids from the city and we ate in a huge dining hall.
(There was a photograph of what we were doing in the 'Daily Telegraph' newspaper clipping, in fact there is a picture of me distributing hot water bottles to the bedrooms, as these buildings were not equipped for winter.)

The one thing which made a great impression on me was the machine in the kitchen. This is where the attendant could place what looked like a yard long bread, on which a roller would spread butter before a cutting blade which would cut off a slice and the bread would be advanced to expose the next slice, whilst the previous one was carried away on a conveyor belt.

Every few days, a new bus load of children arrived at this gateway of freedom.. Somehow we could keep busy just maintaining the place and ourselves and entertaining the younger children. Some programmes were organized to fill the afternoons with cultural and English language classes; we saw movies, and on one occasion Sir Samuel Hoare came to speak to us. Time and again an expensive car would drive up, and some well dressed people would alight from it and proceeded to the Administration office.

There they would dig though the ever growing 'life histories' from the camp's young residents and they selected a number of children to be interviewed. For us this meant "Dress Parade" and "Captain's Inspection." We would be then 'looked at' and 'talked to', 'evaluated' and either 'rejected' or 'accepted.' This meant a family would have agreed to take one or two children, into their home, to care for them, bring them up, feed them, clothe them and educate them. Naturally the significance of such a move was not apparent to us then. Yet in retrospect, over fifty years later, and a family man myself, I must say that I often think about these times. It now seems so obvious how generous and altruistic these good people were. Is it not a tremendous obligation, but a huge sacrifice financially and otherwise. They accepted a strange foreign child, to make a home for him, to give him love and affection and to care for him as one's own child?

There were families who had all these good intentions and a desire to be of help, but their financial condition did not permit them to feed another mouth. Those families would agree to take a refugee child in as a foster child, and one of the charitable organisations were set up for that very purpose and they would compensate them for their expenses. Of course, we have also heard of cases where teenage girls were taken in by families as household help or nanny. Some of their maids did not fare well and were taken advantage of; but these cases were relatively few.

There were also cases where people were financially able and eager to help those refugees in the Lido; yet their way of life and their dwellings were not designed to house small fry. In a number of cases some of these people would put their best efforts together and organize a hostel under a competent leader. They would then take on a group of children of similar background and age and care for them under one roof. One of these hostels was organized by the hastily formed Bournemouth Refugee Committee, and I was fortunate enough to have been amongst those selected to benefit from their generosity. All in all I was there for 10 days and I don't recall the details other than being interviewed to be among their potential 'inmates' for about a dozen boys to stay in a rented small 'Summer Camp' in Swanage which was used by the local Boy Scouts.

Before I left my mother's cousins home, Grete Hirschmann, who was living in London she paid me a visit after she was notified that I was on the first Kindertransport and she decided to pay me a visit. Amazingly I even had a photograph taken in front of a bed of roses, which was an unexpected sight during winter in the UK as we only got to see roses in April in Germany, when the snow melted.

2 Swanage

During the second week of December about ten days after our arrival in England we embarked on a train trip which took us clear across the isle of the Southern coast. It was dark already when we arrived in Swanage, we took a hike through the friendly streets of that small Dorset town and up a steep grassy hill. There we found comfortably heated cabins in the Rotary camp, which during its seasonal inactivity were designated to house our small troop. A cook had been hired to prepare our meals, and a warden (in America you would call him a counsellor,) was to supervise our activities. There was a thrill in making a camp cosy for our wintery stay, in meeting a new set of people, in getting acquainted with a new town. But as the weather was suddenly unusually cold, the romantic aspects of this situation could not melt the ice which formed on the kitchen's water pipes, which could not warm the cabins whose oil heaters could not withstand the exceptionally hard winter.

For a while we tried to keep the camp operational by bringing water up from the nearby hospital, by wearing double layers of clothes and yet even more at night. However shortly before Christmas the situation became unmanageable. Yet no other site could be made available speedily enough to move us on such short notice.

'Swanage Refugee Committee', was a subsidiary of the 'Bournemouth Refugee Committee' and they were responsible for the day to day running of the camp. These people, who were always concerned with our well-being, soon found a way to resolve our predicament. They signed up a group of local citizens to come to our rescue. The next day they came up to the camp, one by one, in their cars each picking up one or more of the frost bound youngsters. I moved in with Mr Hawes who,with his wife and two children occupied a little house at the north end of town, I had a pleasant stay at the Hawes, they had two children Robin and Maggie and I saw an English Christmas and joined in the celebrations on New Years Day. I had a warm cosy little room, a soft bed, good food and a pleasant benevolent atmosphere. I remember on the very first morning I was absolutely startled as Mrs Hawes approached my bed with a cup of tea. I really witnessed a Christmas Celebration. They didn't have a Christmas tree but an advent wreath with candles which was suspended from the ceiling which they lit on Christmas Eve and sang hymns.

I got to know their friends like Roger Brown and Dr Woodroffe and they became my friends. I met all the other folks who housed my fellow hostlers, and all the other folks who made up the committee which looked after our well being who by then busy trying to find another place which could serve as a hostel.

I met many more people than whose names I can recall today. There was Dr Woodroffe of 12 Rempstone Road, and the Mayor Captain Patterson, there were the Gilpin Brown's, and my good friend Roger Browne. From nearby Corfe Castle there was Miss Madeleine West (Although Rick called her Geraldine west so we aren't sure what her first name was.) and Simon; there was a lady who had a pottery and Reverend and Mrs Horan. From Bournemouth there was Mrs Cohn and Mr Carter, Rabbi Chaim Leib Helipern.

There were dozens more, rich people and poor ones, people from all walks of life, going to all different kinds of churches, bachelors, spinsters, childless couples and large families, they all made their contributions to make us establish our home in our 'new haven.'

Shortly after New Year's Day we all bade our 'foster parents' goodbye and moved into our new hostel, Kings Gairn, which was a beautiful place. A large, one family house temporarily vacant, located high upon the cliffs with a magnificent view of Swanage Bay, the Channel and the Isle of White at the Horizon. Mr and Mrs Ellington, an American couple, looked after us in the hostel, and they were soon joined by Mr Phil Carter, a school teacher and a scoutmaster. They really built up a home for us.

They helped us give to our rooms a home like atmosphere, they procured books and games for us, taught us the English language, and English songs and games. But in-spite of all their endeavours they couldn't keep us sufficiently occupied. Man's greatest demoralizing agent, idleness, made itself felt in the house. Again we had to go to the people of Swanage for help. Again they found the answer, we were given a chance to work. Obviously at our age none of us possessed any skills and thus our employment didn't rob anybody of a job, and yet we had the chance to keep busy. Some of us worked in garages, others in stores, one fellow worked in a solicitors office as a run around, whilst another one a barber's help.

Our life became fuller as we worked, met more people, made more friends, as we learned the language of the country I had a little spending money to buy a few thing to go to the picture's as we took walks and learned to love the Dorset countryside.

3.Garage work

Dean and Son Garage Swanage where Alfred Batzdorf would volunteer (photo taken from page 160 of Swanage Past)

I myself worked at the garage of 'Dean and Son', helping with the annual overhaul of the engines and a fleet of touring buses, helping with the pumping gas, you must put the nozzle on the hose in the opening to the gas tank in the car and squeeze the handle. Your job was to exercise the pumping handle 'to and fro,' which was to fill one of these bottles with gasoline, and pull another handle to empty its contents into the auto - mobiles tank, whilst filling the other gas bottle to repeat the process, at that time there was no mechanised dispenser. Most important was making tea and seeing to it that pot didn't run dry. I really learned a lot there, for I knew next to nothing of automotive engines nor of French picture postcards.

I remember some aspects of mostly opportunities to be exposed to an environment where the English language was the only method of communication. I must have earned a bit of 'pin money', for I was able to buy a second-hand bicycle. I used it primarily for going to work, but later, I remember, we took trips to the nearby countryside. A few months later, another change was forthcoming. For reasons we were not familiar with, or reasons I have since forgotten, the Swanage hostel was to be closed. A new site was selected for us in Bournemouth, a larger town about fourteen miles from Swanage. But before we could move to the new hostel there was another period of homelessnesses. Kings Gairn had been closed and Bournemouth was not yet ready. Again some of the Swanage families opened up there homes to us. This time it was our friend Roger Brown who offered a group of us asylum.
Mr Brown was a rich bachelor, who offered up a splendid house high up on a cliff

over looking the channel. His parents he told us were aboard the Titanic when it went down and he inherited a substantial fortune. His mansion had many rooms and his heart was full of charity,

During the summer months Roger would invite groups of underprivileged city children from London to share his luxurious dwelling place; he would give them a chance to breathe clean air, would feed them well and but them new clothes. When one group of boys left, another group came and he looked after them as well. Now he extended his considerable benefits to us. We took hikes and drives through the countryside, played games and listened to his interesting stories and he referred to us as the '7 Dwarfs', although I believe we were more than Seven. The boys called me 'Latsch' which meant big in German and Uncle Roger caught on and called me Large.

We must have stayed with Uncle Roger for several weeks and I remember that we drove around in his open convertible, a ford, that was fitted with an oversized rumble seat, so he could carry more people. It was this time when I developed a special friendship with Kurt Eisenbach and remained friend for a long time.

We even visited him years later when we travelled to England by this time he was called Kurt Ellington and was be now an 'Army Veteran' and a father but sadly he was unwell. But soon this vacation came to end end as the Bournemouth Refugee Committee were looking for permanent accommodation for us and as soon a hostel was ready for us, and we moved to Bournemouth.

THE PINES HOTEL
SWANAGE

Kings Gairn that became a part of Pines Hotel and Clovelly Cottage. The Pines Hotel was refurbished in the 1970's and parts of theses two buildings were demolished as apart of the refurbishment plan.

'Rabbi Chaim Leib Heilpern of the Hebrew Orthodox Synagogue Bournemouth'

This is the Bournemouth Orthodox Synagogue website concerning Rabbi Helipern (http://coseti.org/www.oldsynagogues.org/bournemouth_13.htm)

(Rabbi Heilpern was the Rabbi of the Hebrew Orthodox Synagogue, in Bournemouth both before WW2 during and afterwards. He would have been the Rabbi that Alfred would have known and here he found his faith again. Rabbi Heilpern after the war travelled a lot including to Palestine,as it was called then. He died in San Diego USA, in 1974 aged 73, but little is known of his latter life other than he was a Rabbi in Palo alto California.)

4. Bournemouth

At first the new hostel was very much like the one in Swanage and little changed in the way it was run or in the composition of our small group. Yet, the larger town presented opportunities Swanage could not have provided. I remember a young child prodigy violinist in town on a concert tour playing for us in a hostel. His name was Yehudi Menuhin. I remember that incident so well, because of a bit of humiliation connected with it. Mrs Cohen approached me after the concert with the remark:

" Wasn't that marvellous?" and I replied by translating the German "Er hat mir gut gefallen 'into' He enjoyed me very much, a pronouncement which evoked a slight smile on Mrs Cohen's face and a short language lesson which I never forgot."

Mr Felsen who had been hired as an Assistant Warden, conducted services. But at times other than 'High Holy Days,' we could attend the local Synagogue, and when they were able to 'muster a minyan' this was not a voluntary assignment. The services in the little Synagogue in Bournemouth opened my eyes to an entirely new concept of worship service.

I had been accustomed to sit quietly and obediently in the audience of our great Synagogue in Breslau, listening to our superb chasan and suffering through the sermons of our Rabbi where the usually extremely thoughtful message was overpowered by the excessive length of the sermon. Here, I found an active needs participating congregation, each one praying for his or her needs and not dictated to by the power on the Bimah (platform in the synagogue). At strategic times, the chasan (Cantor who leads prayers) would pause and let everyone catch up and join in common prayer where that was called for.

I do remember the shammes, (Shame is the beadle who looks after the running of the service and the administration, plus the responsibilities) with the golden band around his top hat. (I myself the author went to see Rabbi Adrian Jesner in the same Synagogue 2020 and I felt the presence of G-d come over me. I couldn't stop the tears falling from my eyes and down my face, especially when he told me to got to the Arc to pray, Gods presence became stronger and I was deeply humbled. I have never experienced anything like this before.)

The larger town of Bournemouth gave us a better employment possibility. Now we could seek jobs where we could do more than just keep busy and where we could learn a trade, plus building up a reasonable wage. The hotel trade offered a unique opportunity, inasmuch as foreigners did not require a work permit for employment in hotels and guest houses. As soon as we moved to Bournemouth I gained employment at Durley Dean Hotel as an apprentice.

5. Hotel Work

I started out as a dishwasher, and realising that my engineering career would be at best indefinitely postponed but probably never realised. I soon decided to make the hotel business a career at least for the time being. During the evening hours I was able to attend classes at the Bournemouth Municipal College to further my education, which was slated to go into the field of engineering, but was prematurely interrupted by the happening during those eventful years.

My tendency was to combat misery by making even the most tedious job a challenge, by setting goals to work for, by inventing labour saving shortcuts etc. It must have come to the attention of my supervisor for soon I was advanced to the plate room. Here I washed cutlery, and tea pots, coffee pots, and cream pitchers; you name it: anything was silver plated and needed to shine and sparkle. I was even trained how touching stained objects with a piece of tin foil in the steam heated sink full of soda water, made the stain disappear. But the powers that be did not leave me there for long.

After a short stint in the still room where the coffee machine was located, where we made and sandwiches were rolled butter balls for the tables, I was given the job as a night porter. While the money was a good bit better, what I really liked about this assignment was the fact it was my first job where I had contact with the public.

Whilst much of our time was stoking the furnaces, catching and disposing of rats, shining shoes and and making a fire in the innumerable fireplaces in the lounges, we also served drinks in the lounges and carried luggage for the late arrivals. Thus these contacts with the travelling public also augmented my income in the form of tips.

I remember serving drinks at the New Years party, an annual event staged for the wealthier folks living in that part of the town, as well as vacating guests. I was in the kitchen, when suddenly the dining room doors opened and a couple of men dragged in a totally 'sozzled' guest and they provided a pail so the drunkard could relieve himself of some of liquid he had consumed right here in the kitchen of the four star hotel.

After that accomplishment, assisted by some of his friends, a team of waiters and his wife, the head waiter called me over and ask that I help the wife to escort the husband home who lived only a few streets away. I did as requested and when we arrived at the house we could do no more than plonk the 'wino' down on the first sofa where he immediately passed out. Trying to seize an unexpected moment, the wife tried desperately to have me salvage the evening for her, I never ran so fast back to the hotel in all my life.

After the New Year I served another short stint as a day porter, and then lo and behold, I was taken inside the holy portals called the "Dining Room." I had become a waiter! Albeit a commies waiter, who in USA is called a bus boy. It was clean work and though theoretically one also was supposed to eat the staff meals served in the staff dining room, no waiter ever did. We always managed to subvert some of the morsels which were destined for the dining room.

I remember one room mate who had come from Cyprus and supplemented his income by working as a 'gigolo' to be a companion to elderly ladies. However he was unsuccessful in trying to encourage me to join him! On another occasion when I was sick the hotel a management arranged for a doctor to see me and his name was doctor Risk. This was because as a part of my employment was to be a beneficiary of the Government National Health Insurance System, which Dr Risk inspected wanting assurance he would be paid. (I have still got this document)

6.Trying to save the family

About four months must had gone by since I had left the home of my parents.
Almost a year earlier, my father had registered for Visas for his family to enter the
United States of America as immigrants and our names had been placed on the
waiting list.
Immigration United States was controlled by very strict quota regulations, and only
a limited number of people from any one country were admitted monthly.

A year later, whilst I was living in England, my father, mother, and brother
(who was then 10 years old) where still waiting for their quota number to be called
up, so that they would be free to leave Germany the country of bondage, even though
Washington was anti immigration. Yet over all these months, their life grew more
difficult, the restrictions became harsher, and the world situation grew worse with
war looming on the horizon. It was obvious that, should that come to pass, it would
make their immigration impossible, and ending with a very sad inevitable ending.

These were the ideas transmitted to me in (camouflage) in the letters I received
from home, these ideas and the importance of trying to find for them an intermediary
haven, a place that they could go to wait in peace and security for the time that they
would be admitted to the United States.

There was a young fellow in our hostel, Edward Merkel from Saxony, and one day
he received a visit from his uncle, Mr Jackson from Manchester who became a good
friend to all of us. He took us to a restaurant for tea and took us to the movies where
we saw our first American picture, the Hitchcock thriller "the Lady Vanishes"
(I didn't not understand a thing they spoke about it was in English.)After the outing,
we got to talking about our life and our future, our past, and our families. Mr Jackson
was very patient and listened to what we had to say with great interest.

He became quite intrigued by my endeavour to find a temporary shelter for my
family, and questioned me as to the conditions which would govern such a move.
I told him that I had to make inquiries and was told that it would take somebody to
underwrite a persons livelihood for the duration of his stay in England to get his
permission to come on a temporary (transient) visa.

I do not think that it was more than a week after Mr Jackson went back to
Manchester when I received a letter from him stating that he has verified the
information I had given him and that he was willing and able to guarantee the stay
in England for one member of my family. This was great news. This was a
marvellous showing of their generosity of a comparative stranger, who was in no
way obliged to save my family out of their misery. It struck deep into ones heart and
in retrospect it still does today.

Of course this action stimulated my activities on behalf of my parents, for how could I possibly find a haven, find salvation for one and leave the other one to an uncertain fate? And yet if I talk of "activities" and "endeavours" on my part, I am taking too much credit, for I could not go begging or pleading with people. All I could was make conversation of my situation. But it was proven, you do not have to go begging to truly generous people; they help where they see help is needed, without being asked for it.

Thus it happened that one afternoon I received a visit from a gentle lady, from nearby Corfe Castle, a Miss Madeleine West, who I recall was the mayor of the little town. She had been a member of the Refugee Committee and through them became acquainted with us and our fate, What Miss West had to tell me was by far exceeding any predictable development. She told me that a group of her friends in her home town had agreed to pool amongst themselves money for the guarantee for a member of my family to come to UK. This was on the basis of certain pledges for periodic contributions, to underwrite the guarantee to satisfy the requirements of the Home Office. My feelings of appreciation and gratitude at that time are far beyond anything that I could put into words today. I was moved beyond description.

Now, our warden (councillor) Phil Carter had a lady friend who was a headmistress (principal) of a boarding school. Mr Carter was willing to intercede on my behalf with that lady, and very soon thereafter I was notified that the school had agreed to accept my brother for a reduced fee to cover some of his expenses The stage was set by my work was no means done. Now there started a series of feverish activities in writing letters to the 'Home Office', going to London for interviews, filling in forms and getting signatures.

There was one thing that I would not allow to happen, that with all the cards in my hand, further development on the other side of the channel would thwart the possibilities to save my family. We started race with time. One June morning however, I stood at the docks of Southampton and kissed my father, mother and brother welcome to the shores of freedom, to a great country, whose generous citizens brought about that moment,

My father and brother arrived with merely hand luggage. All their belongings, furniture, house hold goods, clothes, as well as my fathers surgical and urological instruments, were carefully packed in 'lifts', the large containers suitable for loading onto sea - going freighters. The 'Riechsflucht Steuer'(escape tax) of 100% of the estimated value of the goods had been paid, as was a years storage and the cost of freight to the US. Having passed exit inspection, the 'lifts' were stored in the International zone of the harbour of Hamburg. Little did my parents know but that two days after they left the country the 'lifts' were opened and their entire contents were auctioned off.

**Alfred's brother Ulrich on the left, his Mother in the middle,
Alfred is on the right.**

7. The family is Safe

   My parents and brother arrived with passports which had three distinctive features
they were adorned by a big 'J' indicating the bearers of Jewishness. They were
declared invalid after their exit from Germany (i.e. not suitable for re-entry
or for any other purpose); and they contained the revised spelling of Batzdorf
(with one "F"). The story behind this is of interest and bears re telling for the sake
of those who maybe confused by the divergent spelling which the story starts with
father Abraham, widely recognised as the first Jew. When he became a Jew G-d told
him that he would no longer be Abram, but he would henceforth be known as
Abraham. Following that example, it became a custom for converts to Judaism to
change their names (a bit). It seems to have become the custom(at least in some
geographic areas and in some periods of history), for other converts to follow that
custom. Thus, when my grandfather Albert Batzdorf converted to Judaism, he
changed his name to Batzdorff and henceforth all Jewish Batz..'es' were 'dorffs'.Then
along came the Nazis, realising that some Jews with 'Jewish sounding' names had
changed their names to more neutral ones, they ordered all who had changed their
names within the past two generations, to revert to the original spelling of their
family names. Thus, ironically the Batzdorff had to change the <u>Jewish</u> version of their
name to the former <u>non Jewish</u> spelling .

This all happened after I left Germany, so I retained the name I was born with. While I assumed that my father would have abandoned the Nazi ordained spelling of his name eventually (when he was a US citizen), Rick told me years later that father was always disappointed that I had not changed my my name to conform to theirs. Actually, that had never entered my mind, and had he expressed that desire, I may well have conformed to it.

My friends, the Hawes, who at an earlier occasion had so generously housed me in the Swanage Hostel, had now offered me assistance again. They invited my family and me to stay at their home for a couple of weeks, so that we would have chance to talk to each other and celebrate our reunion. Later I went back to work in Bournemouth, and on my days off I went to see my parents, who rented a furnished room in Swanage. Father and mother met many of my old friends and they were well received and felt happy in their new environment.

Father earned some extra money by giving German lessons to a group of school teachers and mother did some needlework and gave some singing lessons, but the main part of their upkeep consisted of the weekly contribution of £1. Each from Mr Jackson and from good people of Corfe Castle. £2 went on room rent and the £1 was used for food. From my meagre earnings I met the expense my brother incurred at school and a little additional gift for my parents from time to time. The family was rescued, the family was settled, the family was happy.

Sometime later my brother Ulli (Rick) was very unhappy in his school in Bournemouth and somehow I was able to transfer Ulli to a school in Swanage called 'Hillcrest' and this was much better for him, there he could see his parents every Sunday. For one thing, he liked the school and the teachers were much better, plus he adored the headmaster and his wife who took an extraordinary liking to him.

Our parents lived right across from the church, and on Sunday mornings, when all the boys were marched to church, Rick joined the march through town in his uniform and when they arrived at church, Ulli was allowed to go to his parent's home instead.. He also went to Garfield school in Langton Matravers.

When I had a day off I would cycle to Swanage, and once in a while my rota made Sunday my day off. I would then leave for Swanage early, so I could witness the entire procedure and then join the family for a reunion. I loved my bike trips to Swanage, when the tides were low, I could abbreviate the journey, by biking on the compact sand at the edge of the water, with the waves lapping at my wheels. Then I would also think these waves would connect me across the seas.

8.Trying for an Instrument apprenticeship

WHERE ALFRED WORKED AT SANDBANKS HOTEL.

Sometime between New Year and Easter I changed jobs. Having been promoted from 'Commies Waiter' several weeks earlier, I was now employed as a 'Demi Chef' (French for half a waiter). As such I found half a better job, in more pleasant surroundings at the Sandbanks hotel in Poole Harbour. Here I did not have to sleep on a cot in the airless basement room. This hotel had actually had a small house set aside solely to house the live in staff. We were about three or four to a room and since this trade was open to foreigners, they proliferated here. Thus our little house was veritable forerunner of the United Nations, and I loved the friendly atmosphere there. Yet I was getting great money by then,and I enjoyed my work. I realised that my life's ambition was not satisfied by this endeavour. I had always been interested in physics, and especially mechanics, and I had always been good in handicrafts, in the use of tools.

Summing up my interests and skills, I realised I should make my career in engineering or an allied profession or trade. During the evening hours I was able to attend 'Bournemouth Municipal College' to further my education in engineering but sadly I couldn't go far in this because of what was going on all around me including the beginnings of WW2.Thus when one Sunday morning I found an advertisement in the 'Daily Telegraph', where a surgical instrument maker and inventor was looking for an apprentice. I wrote a letter to the gentleman who offered the position and I told him in detail about my background and the necessity for me should I become eligible for the position to procure a 'work permit.' This was an overture of another example of English Charity.

Soon after I answered the advertisement I received a letter from Mr Davies in Cardiff inviting me to come there for an interview. Looking back I found that this was not an unwarranted demand, that a fellow who wants to hire a helper should wish to meet him before he makes up his mind. Yet in my precarious situation I felt forced to reply to him that I had neither the money for the trip to Wales, nor could I afford to lose a couple of days pay at my present job. In an answer to my letter I received a bus ticket from Mr Davies, and an assurance that a hotel room had been reserved for me and paid for.

This moved me very much, and had I not already been acquainted with the English concept of unselfishness, this most certainly been a fine introduction to it. I went to Cardiff the following week and I arranged to take a day off work and used the Royal midnight bus to get to get to my destination only to find that Mr Davies had been called out of town and learned later he had sent me a telegram to say he had to go to London to utilize his products in a surgical procedure. Mrs Davies however received me very well, and invited me for lunch at her house, had a fine talk, and got well acquainted.

After my return home, I had hardly time to mourn my seemingly unsuccessful trip when I received a commination from Mr Davies that on the judgement of his wife he would be happy for me to join his company. He was willing to give me spending money for fifteen shillings a week while I learned. Again my conscious hurt me greatly.

There was a splendid opportunity for me, as there was a man who put a lot of trust in me though he had never met me (by paying my trip to Wales) before he had even seen me. He had financially assisted me, and yet I felt forced to tell him that I could not accept his offer of a position, The remuneration he offered could not suffice to pay for my upkeep, and I was obliged to pay for my brother's school a certain sum in addition to what I needed myself, fifteen shillings would never do. But Mr Davies would not take "No" for an answer. He talked the case over with his wife and wrote to me that they had decided to room, and board me at their house (free of charge) in addition to the fifteen shilling payment. This was the greatest generosity I ever saw an employer extended to one of his men. Together with Mr Davies I applied for a 'work Permit,' and had the process of procuring that paper being an expedient one, I might still be associated wit this great man. Yet, as it turned out, it took many months of a tiresome wait, and yet no answer from the Labour Department had been received. In the meantime my parents were mortified that the time had come that they would be admitted to the United States, and thus they could no longer make use of their transition visa for residence in the United Kingdom, as my endeavour to procure working papers seemed so hopeless, I notified Mr Davies that I felt compelled to give up the idea of building up my career in England, and decided to join my parents on their trip to the United States, though my future was quite uncertain in these dark time. Our plans were determined, and all necessary arrangements made. Late in May 1940, we packed our meagre belongings for our trip to Liverpool, to embark our ship to USA.

The day before we left I received a letter from the Ministry of Labour that my 'work permit' had been granted. Heading for a new and uncertain haven, I looked back from the boat to the English shoreline. I felt a deep emotion, full of gratitude, and respect to a great and splendid country, to an unselfish, and charitable people, to a great group of friends whom I considered the guardian of democracy."

A drawing of St Marys Church in Swanage.

Lotte Batzdorf, Alfred's mother drew this Sketch of St Mary's Church, Swanage, in 1940 from a window across the street from St Marys's in Milbrook. A lady called Doreen sent the sketch to Rick Batzdorf many years later.

Susanne & Alfred Batzdorff

Alfred was married to Susanne Biberstein who was born in 1921, and thy met as children in Breslau, Germany which is now Wroclaw, Poland. Her parents were both physicians, and after Jews lost their licenses to practice medicine in 1938, her immediate family made the decision to emigrate to the United States. Alfred and Susanne met again when Alfred, and his family moved to USA, and they had both lost many members of their extended families who were not able to leave Europe before the Holocaust.

In 1944 Susanne and Alfred got married and at this time Alfred joined then the Navy, whilst Susanne became a librarian, and raised their three children. They lived in New York, Delaware, and then Pennsylvania before settling in Santa Rosa in 1982. Alfred became a mechanical engineer something he always wanted to do, whilst Susanne always wanted to became a writer.

**Suzanne's Aunt Edith Stein, a 'Carmelite Nun'
Murdered in Auschwitz and Canonized as Saint Teresa of the Cross.
Both Saint of Europe, and Auschwitz.**

Alfred's wife soon became a published author, and translated her Aunt Edith's publications and wrote a book called 'Aunt Edith'. Edith was born in Breslau, Poland, in to a Jewish family in 1891, and became a very outstanding pupil. Edith was in fact the very famous Carmelite nun who despite being baptized as a Roman Catholic in 1922 in Cologne Cathedral, and was sent to Carmel Echt Holland, was arrested by the Germans when they invaded Holland with her sister Rose.

In 1942 the sisters were murdered in the gas chambers of Auschwitz because of their Jewish background, despite Edith's conversion. After Edith's death she was named St Teresa Benedicta of the Cross when she was beatified in 1987 by Pope John Paul II. Edith was also later Canonised in 1997 and is the Saint of both Europe and Auschwitz.

In Warner Max Corden's book 'Lucky Boy in the Lucky Country' it says on page 206 it says, "Ulrich Batzdorf 'Rick' Batzdorf was my best friend at school in Breslau. He and his family left Breslau in 1939, he spent a year in boarding school in England (Swanage) (like me) and then in 1940 he and his family moved to the USA. He and I corresponded regularly between Melbourne and New York in our teenage and college and university years. Eventually we lost contact.

Years later, I met someone who told me that Rick had moved from New York to Los Angeles (LA).Travelling often to USA and Melbourne, during one of my LA stop overs, I found his name in the LA phone book, and hence made contact. They lived in Santa Monica. After that Dorothy and I stayed with Rick and his wife Ellen during our LA stopovers , and an old friendship was renewed. Rick gad met Ellen in England. It is amazing how we four related so easily. Among other things we seemed to have the same political views. Rick is professor of Neurosurgery at the university of California at Los Angeles(UCLA) Hospital, now (2016) partially retired."

Max and his mum   **Max and his wife Dorothy**

Chapter 9

"Crack of the Pistol"
By F. S Horan
Taken from page 22

Repercussions from Munich were not long coming. Through a rent in sheep's clothing which Hitler had put on, a wolfs head poked out. On 'Armistice Day' that year of all days, we read of "Shocking treatment to the Jews in Germany" This terrible massacres of the unfortunate people. As many as could get away fled the country. For those thousands of refugees (some here in England) Lord Baldwin made a very moving broadcast appeal for help.

In Swanage we did what we could, and a whole lot of Jewish refugee boys (forty, I think) where put into a summer camp on the downs to the south of the town. It was December, and to make matters worse for them, the weather on their arrival was arctic, with a strong North Easterly blowing. It was bitterly cold, snowing hard, water pipes, everything frozen up. It would have meant death for the boys to be left in that exposed camp on the downs.

Something had to be quickly, but where to house them was the question. After hurried enquiries we were told of a suitable large house near the Grand Hotel which had been unoccupied sine the death of lady Portal, and now belonged to miss Portal, a sister of Mrs Guy Russell. Colonel and Mrs Russell, got in touch with her somehow and at once the house was put into our disposal. Late that same night we housed all the Jewish boys there.

Several men of Swanage Urban Council and various helpers, male, and female. Muriel and I among them, spent many hours warming up the cold empty house, lighting fires in every bedroom dragging damp mattresses in front of them, fetching blankets helping to settle the boys in. Authors note (this place was called Kings Gairn which with Clovelly Cottage which became the Pine hotel)

Amongst the Jewish Refugees who came to Swanage at this time was a certain Dr and Mrs. Alfred Batzdorf and their family, They were anxious to get to the United States. But it was a long time before they could get visas. We were able to help them in this matter and in other ways. They are now happily settled in New York where Dr Batzdorf has a flourishing practice and the sons are doing extremely well. We hear each Christmas from Dr, and Mrs Batzdorf.

Chapter 10
Rev F.S. Horan
'Crack of the Pistol'

I once interviewed Author Jason Tomes, on my radio show 'Lunchtime with Elaine' and he writes many books about Swanage. In conversation he told me "I came across information in the 'Western Gazette' newspaper and 'From the Crack of the Pistol' (1955), a memoir by F. S. Horan (who had been a track athlete in his youth; hence the title) An issue of the "Western Gazette" from January 1939 carried an appeal for donations of bed linen for the refugees living at Kings Gairn.

Kings Gairn along with Clavell Cottage became Pine Hotel which was refurbished in 70's and it lost most of Kings Gairn and Clavell Cottage in the process. Kingsgarn had for many years been the holiday home of the Portal family from London. I also have a note that the 'principal' at Kings Gairn was Philip Carter, a former pupil of Oldfield School in Swanage who had become a teacher in Bath. (I don't know where this info came from.) Presumably, Kings Gairn functioned like a boarding school while the boys were there."

In Rev. Horan's book 'Crack of the Pistol' he often spoke about 'Forres School' where he was a teacher for a while. On page 196 it reads:-

"To Forres I owe many lasting friendships not only to those who are now 'Old Forresian's,' but with papas and mommas who brought their young hopefuls to the school while Muriel and I functioned there."

Later on in the same page 196 it reads:-
"Some boys leave their prep school behind them with no hankering ever to see it again. That can't be said of Forres boys that are keen to revisit their old school, laugh over old times with 'Chaddy' and tell them of their present doings and difficulties, and triumphs.

A Forresian re-union Luncheon is held annually in London where 'Old Forresian's' drink to their health to the 'Chaddies', and the school, and all Forresian's past, and present. The spirit of Forres school is well expressed in the school song, which I insert here by permission. It was composed by Arthur Chadwick, the founder of Forres School."

From 'Crack of the Pistol'
Rev. F . S Horan.
<u>Forres School Song</u>

Boys of Forres sun or rain,
Struggle on with might and main;
Do you duty ne'er complain;
Faint Not ! Sons of Forres.
Fear disdaining, play the game;
Ever spotless be your name ;
Brothers all to win fair fame;
Be ye Sons of Forres.
Let no slacker mar your ranks;
Give no rotter place nor thanks;
Idle folly feeble pranks.
Scorn ye sons of Forres.
Cheerful steadfast running straight,
Stifle envy malice hate;
Falsehood that could devastate;
Crush ye, Sons of Forres.
Dally not in work nor play;
be not glum but ever gay;
Weal or woe you must delay;
Courage Sons of Forres.

By Arthur Chadwick

Picture of Forres School Swanage.

Rev. Fredrick Seymour Horan,was an international athlete in his Cambridge days, and he was the first man to run 3 miles in the Inter Varsity sports in 15 minutes, Cambridge University students still remember Fredrick as the greatest athletes ever, Later on he became a partner with Arthur Chadwick, at Forres school and he mentions how he, and others in Swanage helped move the Jewish refugees to Kings Gairn from a local holiday camp as the boys arrived in a very cold winter. Later on Rev. Fredrick Seymour Horan, became chaplain at Naval College in Osborn House, Isle of Wight.

C.U.A.C First Strings 1894.

Rev. Fredrick Seymour Horan first left on the middle row.

Rev. F. S. Horan, was a very amazing and kind man who lived, an exciting life, and he made a great impression on the young Alfred Batzdorf, plus his parents who kept in touch with Fredrick, and Muriel for many years.

Chapter ll
Gary Saul 'Maier's Boy'
By Craig Saul.

Craigs Mum Joan & Dad Gary Saul

Craig Saul

He never knew his Hebrew name. Or perhaps he simply forgot it over time, in the same way that he left behind his family, friends and religion when he came to this country. He did, however, know his father's Hebrew name, which was Maier. And, so, he was Maier's Boy.

My father was born in Berlin in 1924. His given name was Günther Saul, although he later anglicised his first name to Gary. Like many others, he never hid his personal experiences of 1930s Germany, but neither did he openly talk about them unless asked. He did share very broad-brush memories of the segregation that was evident in public places, as well as the day he was told by his teacher that he was no longer welcome in his school and would have to find an alternative place of education. But that was largely as far as he went in terms of talking about "the dark days".

What I do know was that, by whatever means his family managed to find, he was fortunate to be part of the very first Transport of 196 Kinder that left Berlin and arrived in Harwich on the TSS Prague on December 2nd 1938. At 14 years of age, he was one of the eldest children to make that trip.

The children were initially housed at the Warner's Holiday Camp in nearby Dovercourt – later used, in much happier circumstances, for location filming for the BBC comedy "Hi-de-Hi!" some 40-odd years later. Because of the media interest in the very first refugee arrivals, he was captured in both newsreel and still footage taken at the time. Photographs taken on-board the Prague – he is the boy in the cap in the image below – show him and others looking totally disconsolate, and later featured in both Picture Post magazine and as the inspiration for an advert to raise funds for the Lord Baldwin Fund for Jewish refugees. Although the photos portray complete dejection, the additional reality was that the overnight sea crossing from the Hook of Holland had been an extremely rough one, and many of the Kinder were rather seasick.

Photos and brief newsreel footage taken outside the holiday chalets in Dovercourt, meanwhile, have found their way into the landmark documentary "Into the Arms of Strangers" as well a commemorative placard close to the site itself. My father is the sixth child from the left, waving his left hand.

The registration slip held by the Central British Fund for German Jewry (CBF) at Bloomsbury House in London details him as Home Office Permit Holder No.43, and shows him as having left Dovercourt two weeks after his arrival in this country for the Dorset Rotary Camp in Swanage. My father occasionally referenced his feelings of rejection at being one of the very last children selected by prospective foster parents. Unsurprisingly, the little girls and younger Kinder in general went first. He was older – already a man in the Jewish religion – as well as tall and gangly.

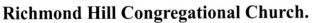

Richmond Hill Congregational Church.   **4 Portarlington Road Bournemouth.**

Fortunately, however, he found the perfect home. He was fostered by Ethel Anne Mooring Aldridge who came from Swanage, and who features elsewhere in this book and is described as "a lady of independent means" in the 1939 register, with a chauffeur, gardener and housekeeper in her employment. He lived with her at 4 Portarlington Road in Bournemouth, later attending Richmond Hill Congregational Church to receive Christian teaching. He remained a Christian for the rest of his life. While not all Kinder had such positive experiences with their foster parents, my far country he became an Anglophile for life – and absolutely adored Miss Aldridge as his foster parent, regarding her as a true saint. Even in his later life, he always referred to her as "Miss Aldridge" as an obvious mark of respect.

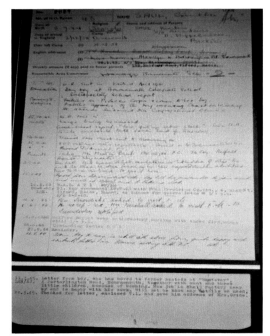 

Gary Saul's Kindertransport Papers.   **'Roger Brown'**

At some point, he also came into contact with the "Roger Brown" who also appears in this book, and they maintained a friendship that lasted a lifetime. I never met Mr Brown, but received the occasional book as a birthday or similar present, always signed as "Uncle Roger" in a flourishing writing style with a fountain pen.

My father received a place at Bournemouth Collegiate School, although having to take lessons in what was then clearly a second language must have been an early handicap. There is reference in his CBF registration slip to his school reports being "satisfactory" and "good…. but getting rather slack".

Amazingly, his English teacher, a gentleman named Norman Field, was - some 35 years later - my French teacher at Poole Grammar School. I recall by dad also recounting the occasion when he attended a garden fete in Bournemouth that was opened by a very special dignitary in Haile Selassie, the Ethiopian emperor being in exile in England following the invasion of his country by Italy.

Any additional reader insights on either the Bournemouth Collegiate School or the occasion of the fete would be very much appreciated, as I have little else to go on. My dad was one of the lucky ones in that he was re-united separately with both his parents. At some point between December 1938 and the declaration of war, my grandfather managed to escape Germany and reach Britain, subsequently fighting for the Allies in the Pioneer Corps, and being at Dunkirk during the 1940 evacuation.

Meanwhile, my grandmother – who had originally converted to Judaism in order to marry his father – quietly converted back after a divorce and amazingly spent the War untouched in Germany, only leaving Berlin after the Russians moved in and before the Wall went up. One day, she loaded as many possessions as she could into two bags, put on multiple layers of clothing and simply walked across the border. She never looked back at the property and life she left behind. My father's aunt and uncle also escaped to Britain, while a few additional relatives made it to the US. Those left behind were not so lucky.

My dad always retained a close connection and draw to Bournemouth, Swanage and Dorset in general. Although later emigrating to the United States in the early 1950s and starting a family, he very much returned to his roots when moving the family back to England in 1973, living in Poole, working in Bournemouth and also rekindling his friendship of 30 years earlier with Roger Brown.

He also started writing what proved an uncompleted narrative of his arrival in this country, under the title of "Maier's Boy" that I have used to dedicate this chapter. With my father's passing in 2011, I have, in a way, become the keeper of the Kindertransport flame in my family, and would like to thank several parties here. Firstly, my wife Carol, for her Ancestry research, records and general sleuthing to better piece my father's story together. I have also received help and friendship from the Harwich Museum, which has a special display dedicated to the Kindertransport and offers annual talks on the subject. I have been lucky enough at one of those presentations to meet the son of a girl who, like my father, arrived on that very first Kindertransport. We bonded immediately.

I have also been very fortunate to correspond with the author of this book, Elaine Merrikin Trimlett Glover, whose relative Irma Zanker was one of the eight adults who accompanied that very first Kindertransport. I therefore now have the names of eight more people my father no doubt engaged with on that life-defining trip. Through this book and additional correspondence, Elaine has also provided invaluable information on Miss Aldridge and Roger Brown. These relationships mean the world to me. We have a special connection because of our shared history. It cannot go away.

Chapter 12

Trevor Chadwick and Sir Nicholas Winton
Kindertransport project.

Trevor Chadwick was born on 22nd April 1907, and died 23rd December 1979 aged 82. He attended University where he was the captain of a rugby team, and graduated in 1928. After graduating, he joined the Colonial Service, working in Nigeria for 18 months after which he became a Latin teacher at his father's school called Forres in Swanage, Dorset. In January 1939, Trevor travelled to Czechoslovakia with a fellow teacher from Forres, Mr Geoff Phelps, to accompany two refugee children back to Britain including Peter Walder, Willie Weigl and a young girl called Henrietta, and although she much younger than Geoff, later became his wife and mother to Guy Phelps.

Trevor, whilst in Prague, met a female refugee child called Gerda Mayer, and after he interviewed both Gerda and her family, he took Gerda on a plane back to Swanage with the Gerda's friend Hannah Stern, who travelled with Gerda and on arrival to the UK went to live with other another guarantor from Swanage, Mrs T.W Style, who lived on Ratling Road.

Muriel Chadwick, Trevor's mother, who also worked at Forres school, sponsored Gerda by putting up the guarantee of £50 so she could have permission to admit Gerda into Britain as a refugee. Trevor said about Prague: "We got a clear impression of the enormity of the task. We so often saw halls of confused refugees and batches of lost children, mostly Jewish, and we saw only the fringe of it all."

Once back in Swanage with the three refugee children, Trevor returned to Czechoslovakia to help rescue more children and that's when he came across Sir Nicholas Winton. Sir Nicholas Winton, (Jewish last name Werthelm) was born 19th May 1909 – died 1st July 2015. Whilst on a brief visit to Czechoslovakia, he shared what was happening to the Jewish people since the 'night of the broken glass' (kristallnacht) and that the children needed to be rescued. Nicholas returned to the UK to fulfil the legal requirements of bringing the children to Britain and finding homes and sponsors for them after finding a list of children who were in need of rescuing from the Nazi Regime.

In the meantime, Trevor's first job was to evacuate children on a 20-seat aeroplane from Prague, and later they evacuated children by train to Prague railway station and from Prague, the children, with adult escorts including Trevor, journeyed by rail through Poland and then to a seaport in the Baltic where they sailed to Britain. Sir Nicholas Winton back in UK worked hard to get permission for the children to be granted entry. Trevor was more than likely to have been involved with getting children forged documents from the Gestapo and then things became more, and more difficult as the Nazi regime took control of Germany. Refugee workers decided to leave the country, and in early June 1939, however not before Trevor led a final trainload of 123 children, and left Czechoslovakia for the UK.

<u>Sir Nicholas Winton</u>

Nicholas Winton seemed to get more publicity, and exposure about Kindertransport than the others and years later he was honoured by Esther Rantzen on 'That's Life', for his participation in the Kindertransport and Nicholas was also knighted. However he said that Trevor had done the more dangerous work.

Its my own opinion that there were a number of people who did as much as Trevor Chadwick or even more of this dangerous work, such as Florence Nankivell, Doreen Warriner, Robert J. Stopford, Beatrice Wellington, Josephine Pike and many more. In fact they all had a part to play in rescuing the Jewish children and adults. Without their teamwork and bravery <u>ALL,</u> these children would have most likely perished in the concentration camps, gas chambers and ghettos, and their offspring would never had existed.

***A Post Card of Some Of The
669 Kindertransport Children
saved by
Humanitarians
Sir Nicholas Winton
Trevor Chadwick***

Chapter 13

By John Corben
Chairman of the Trevor Chadwick Committee.

"On August Bank Holiday Monday 2022 a life sized bronze statue to a hitherto 'Unsung Local Hero,' was unveiled on the Recreation Ground in Swanage. This was the culmination of some two and a half year's hard work by a group of dedicated residents who wanted to honour the memory of Trevor Chadwick.

Trevor Chadwick was a teacher at a local 'Boarding School' called Forres. Trevor was tasked by the school to go to Prague in late 1938 to bring back two children so that they could be brought up in safety in Swanage. He was so moved by the plight of other children whilst in Prague that he returned for a period of 6 months and during that time was responsible for saving the lives of a total of 669 children.

Trevor's exploits only came to light a few years ago and it was thought that a permanent memorial should be placed in a prominent position in the town recognising his bravery and determination. I was pleased to be involved with the group as I felt something of an affinity with Trevor. He had served on the Swanage Lifeboat for a few years and I had done exactly the same some 40 years later. The lifeboat community in Swanage is a very close knit family and I felt that this would honour Trevor's memory.

My father who had fought in the war, was a D-Day veteran, and he remained in Germany for a year after the cessation of hostilities. He was instructed by the army to visit Belson concentration camp where he interrogated the guards being a fluent German speaker. He witnessed the horror of the holocaust but never spoke about his experiences. I wanted to honour my father's memory as well as Trevor."

<u>Some of the 'Trevor Chadwick Trust'</u>
<u>Who raised money for Trevor's statue.</u>

Back row; Councillor Bill Trite, Ex-Mayor Mike Bonfield, Mel, (Unknown to me)
Bottom row, The Mayor's husband Les & Mayor of Swanage Tina Foster
Sculptor Moira Purver,
Ex- Mayor Avril Harris
Ex-Magistrate & Chairman of 'Trevor Chadwick Committee' John Corben.

Chapter 14

TALES OF BOURNEMOUTH KINDER
By Josephine, Jackson, Kindertransport Education Officer.

"I have been involved in Kindertransport Education since 2000 and on coming to Bournemouth in 2005 discovered some very interesting local Kinder stories.
One of the earliest kinder I heard about was Alfred Batzdorf's amazing story which has been written about in this book. This was in the Wessex Jewish News as a result of local Councillors, Anne and Michael Filer visiting family in Santa Rosa, USA and meeting Alfred at a synagogue there! When he heard they were from Bournemouth he immediately told them of his early life in Bournemouth and Swanage. They asked him to do an article for the Wessex Jewish News. Like many of the kinder arriving in Harwich, he was sent to Butlins Dovercourt Holiday Camp (on the first transport out of Germany arriving in England on 2nd December 1938).

Alfred was then sent with 20 other boys to Bournemouth to a hostel run by the Bournemouth Refugee Committee, a group of Christian ladies well known in the area, one of them was Miss Mooring Aldridge. They also established a hostel in Swanage where Alfred was sent, which soon had to be abandoned as it was a very cold winter, as well as there being no heating, the windows couldn't be shut! Private individuals agreed to house the boys temporarily.

A friend, Bournemouth born Rhona Taylor, told me the story of Lotte and Herbert Wolff, her future brother-in-law aged seven and his sister, aged thirteen who came on Kindertransport from Frankfurt. They were sent to stay in Branksome Park with Miss Elaine Heggie, a devout Christian lady who also took in a third refugee and became their legal guardian.

The Dorset Register of German Refugees was started in which details of all the children's progress and health was noted. Miss Heggie sent Lotte to Queensmount School and Herbert to Wychwood School in Meyrick Park. He later went to St.

Edwards School in Oxford. All the children had to have a sponsor and a distant relative, Hannah Hale, acted as sponsor for Lotte and Herbert.

By an amazing coincidence, a friend of Rhona's worked at Bournemouth Citizen's Advice Bureau for many years. The manager decided to clear out an old cupboard and pulled out the tattered ledger named 'The Dorset Register of German Refugees'! The manager gave the ledger to Rhona's friend who showed it to Rhona and that is where this information comes from. Tucked into the register was a letter from Hannah Hale asking about the progress of Lotte and Herbert. The register shows that Lotte was very interested in farming and after the war went to work on a farm in Wales. In 1948 she went to work on a kibbutz in Israel and remained in Israel ever since.

When Rhona's sister Doris and Herbert married in Reading the Rabbi asked Elaine Heggie to stand under the Chuppah (a Jewish Wedding canopy) together with Herbert and Rhona's parents, a very moving gesture. The couple have four sons, daughters in law and three grandchildren. (They originally met at the 5705 Youth Club in the Synagogue Hall.) Doris and Herbert took the register to the Wiener Library in London where it is on display in the Holocaust Section. Lotte and Herbert's family all perished in the Holocaust.

Otto Hutter arrived in Harwich on the 12th December 1938 aged fourteen on the 1st Kindertransport out of Vienna with 400 other kinder. He was bussed to Dovercourt and then to a boarding house in Broadstairs for the winter. Later he was moved to a country house near Ipswich where two gentlemen came to sponsor two refugee boys for the private school of which they were Trustees. Otto was chosen and had an amazing career. Aged sixteen he was sent to 'Wellcome Physiological Research Laboratories' as 'war work' as he was now an 'enemy alien.' There under the supervision of several seconded scientists he worked on the refinement of insulin and penicillin. He became a brilliant Professor of Physiology spending the last 20 years of his working life as Regius Professor at the University of Glasgow.
(There is more information about his achievements on Google.)

After retirement he came to Bournemouth and we became great friends. He had a wonderful warm personality with tremendous energy and always a twinkle in his eyes. It was a privilege to call him a friend. He soon discovered another Viennese kinder, Walter Kammerling, who had also retired to Bournemouth. By coincidence they had travelled on the same transport from Vienna! Walter was also a special person, travelling all over the country telling his story mainly to schoolchildren and also at many Holocaust Memorial Day events.

Otto Hutter.   **Otto's identification number**

Otto died in December 2020 aged 96 and Walter in February 2021 aged 97. Both of them lost their parents in the Holocaust as well as many family members. Another amazing Bournemouth story is that of Ruth Levisohn told to me by a member of Bournemouth Hebrew Congregation.

On an afternoon in 2017, when unusually the couple concerned were at home on a weekday, the doorbell rang and seven people stood at the door, an elderly lady, a middle-aged couple, a young couple and two small boys, four generations. They explained that the elderly lady (Ruth now aged 89) lived in their house from 1939 to 1947. They had come from Chicago because Ruth wanted to see the house once more. They had seen the mezuzah (a small box with a parchment inside inscribed with Hebrew verses from the Torah which Jewish people are commanded to fix to the doorpost of their home), and were delighted it was now a Jewish home as Ruth who had come from Germany on Kindertransport, had been taken in by previous owners, a Christian couple Thomas and Grace Ashby who sponsored her and looked after her.

The family were immediately invited in and Ruth asked "is there still a little house at the bottom of the garden where she had played." Indeed, they had a Wendy House in which their children and grandchildren spent many happy hours. Emotionally they held hands and took Ruth to see it. They heard Ruth's story over the next few hours some of which she had never even told her family. She had been cared for with great kindness, and love and playing in the Wendy House had helped her overcome the worry about her parents and older brother who had been left in Germany. She travelled from London to Bournemouth on her own to the Ashby family who had arranged for her to stay with them some months before.

The Ashby's had two daughters and Ruth was sent to Talbot Heath School with them and then onto a Boarding School. Ruth received letters from her parents and brother, and very much later she discovered they had perished in May 1942. In 1947 she sailed from Liverpool to New York aged nineteen as she had discovered some family there. She later moved to Chicago where she married, and the family visiting were 'of course', the result of that marriage.

Our friends were overwhelmed that this elderly lady had travelled 4000 miles 80 years later purely because she had remembered her happy times in this house. It is also a testament to the kindness of the Ashby's. As with the Trevor Chadwick Kindertransport Children, here are some of the stories I discovered through my involvement with the Trevor Chadwick Trust.

Peter Walder came with Trevor and his school teacher colleague on the first Kindertransport out of Prague in January 1939 and was sponsored by Forres Preparatory School in Swanage, Dorset. We contacted Peter's son Paul through the Association of Jewish Refugees, and he told us Peter left England in 1945 to be reunited with his father. Paul, his sister and grandchildren all live in Chile, though Paul emphasised his father always felt English and was eternally grateful for the kindness he had received in Swanage.

Gerda Mayer (nee Stein) came on a flight with 19 other children from Prague and recalled Trevor wiping away her tears. She was sponsored by Trevor's mother and also had very happy memories of Swanage. She was thrilled to hear about the statue to commemorate Trevor even though she was very ill and died in July 2021 having contributed to the funding of the statue.

Gumpel Sisters, Laura, Lisolette (Lilo) and Rosemarie (Romie). Laura's son David from Hove contacted us and told us that the sisters came on the 1st June transport from Prague having fled Berlin with their parents in 1938 and were taken in by a lady in London who took great care of them. He sent a copy of his mother's book 'Three Lives in Transit'. Lilo and Romie emigrated to the USA in the 1950's, Lilo became a radiographer, and Romie head of Art Education at a New York School. Laura married, and had two sons. She did a great deal of voluntary work for the National Health Service.

Lia Lesser, (nee Blum) I was told about Lia by a friend in Bournemouth who was a former Birmingham resident. Aged 8 she came on the biggest transport organised by Trevor Chadwick on 1st July. She went to Nursing College in Birmingham and attended the Synagogue where she met her husband. They have two daughters, and two grandsons. All her family perished. She is still giving talks on her experiences. She told me about going to the Czechoslovakian school in Wales, and put me in touch with another Prague kinder, Milena, (nee Fleischmann) who is a mine of information.

Fleischmann Sisters. Milena aged 10, and Eva aged 3 came on the last train out of Prague on 2ⁿᵈ August 1939. They were taken in by a family in Ashton under Lyme and also went to the Czech Refugee school in Wales. Milena married architect Sir George Grenfell Baines in 1954 and they had a daughter and a son, 4 grandchildren and 4 great-grandchildren. She has had a very busy life, being very involved in the Royal Liverpool Philharmonic Orchestra and Czech issues. She was awarded 'Outstanding Czech Woman of the Year' from GB in 2003. I suggest you look her upon google for fuller information. Eva settled in USA and also married an architect and became a school principal and later a group therapist for adults with long term mental illness.

Tomaschoff Brothers, Felix 12, Willy 9 and Euwin 7. Willy's son Gideon contacted us from Canada through the 'Trevor Chadwick Memorial Trust' website. He told me that that there was nobody to meet the three boys when they arrived in London and a taxi driver took them to a refugee hostel. The boys' parents escaped to Palestine, and in 1949 they were reunited there. Willy and Euwin became lawyers, and judges. Felix went into banking but aged 18 he was killed in one of the Arab wars. Gideon said his father never lost his English accent!

Bournemouth Kinder 1940.
(In the picture is Alfred Batzdorf)

Milenia Grefall Baines talking about her experience of being put on the last train from Prague.

The Photo is credited to Karla Gowlett.

Ruth Levinson visiting the house where she stayed as a Kindertransport child.

Chapter 15
The Unveiling of Trevor Chadwick Statue.

Sculptor Moira Purver

Nick Winton & Samuel Chadwick
Grandchildren of Sir Nicholas Winton & Trevor Chadwick.

Pamela & Rabbi Adrian Jesner   Rabbi Michaels & (Unknown to me)
Ex-Mayor Mike Bonfield

Samuel Chadwick, Richard Drax MP & Councillor Bill Trite.

Chapter 16

Names of the Winton/ Chadwick children sent to the Dorset Area.
Taken From Nicholas Winton's website of list children on the Prague Kindertransport.
https://www.nicholaswinton.com/the-list

Name of Child.	Serial Number.	DOB.	Guarantor.
Roxanne Bauer	7436	18/06/1923	Joy. L Page Dorchester Dorset
Grete Sylvia Bauer	7485	18/06/1923	William Machorton Dorchester
Suse Broll	7747	01/09/1924	F. E Bowman Christchurch
Eva Diamant	8180	01/01/1924	Miss Dunn Sandecote School Parkstone, Poole Dorset.
George Hicky	1625	14/08/1932	Adolfine Glass Dorset looked after by Miss Knight Shroton Dorset
Ernest Lowenthal	12364	05/01/926	Mrs Harding Hampreston Wimborne Dorset
Milena Marie Roth	5869	03/10/1932	C. H. Vernon 91 Wentworth Ave Bournemouth Dorset
Edith Rudinger	15342	02/03/1925	A. J. Elgar Forrest House, Grove Rd. Eastcliff Bournemouth Dorset.
George Schwartz	12438	13/11/1923	Hostel of Bournemouth Committee Angela M. Brownlow Lymington Hant's.
Gerda Stein	4696	09/06/1927	Mrs Chadwick, Fair Meadow B' Stone near Swanage Dorset.
Hanna Stern	4691	21/07/1929	Mrs T. W Style, 42 Ratling Road Swanage Dorset
Eva Vbra	8173	01/06/1924	Sent to Smedmore Towers School Near Kimmeridge / Corfe Castle Dorset.

Chapter 17

Gerda Mayer nee Stein.
9 June 1927 – 15 July 2021

Gerda Kamilla Stein was one of Trevor Chadwick's Kindertransport children he brought back with him from Prague to stay at Forres School, Swanage, Dorset. Gerda was born into a Jewish family and her parents were Erna and Arnold Stern of Karlsbad, Czechoslovakia. Arnold sold ladies coats and dresses and her mother Erna had a knitwear business. In 1938 the family fled to Prague to escape the Nazis and had hoped to emigrate but after chasing officials in emigration, Arnold approached Trevor Chadwick in February 1939, to help rescue his children from the Nazi regime.

Trevor found a place for Gerda on a plane to Britain on 14th March 1939, the day before Nazi troops entered Prague. Gerda's father Arnold was sent to Nisko concentration camp, where he later escaped and joined the Soviet Forces on the Eastern front and died in a Soviet Labour Camp. Gerda's mother was sent to Theresienstadt, Concentration Camp, and died a year later in Auschwitz.

On arrival at Croydon airport Gerda Mayer and another Kindertransport child Hanna Stern, left the other group of refugees from Prague, and drove to Swanage, Dorset, with Hanna's guarantor, Mrs Style, who lived at 42 Ratling Road Swanage. They took Gerda to Forres School to be looked after by Mrs Muriel Chadwick Trevor's mother. whilst Trevor returned back to Prague. Gerda got on quite well with Muriel Chadwick, but having a German accent Gerda was bullied by the other children. In 1942 she moved to Stoatley Rough school, Hazlemere, Surrey when Forres School was in decline. Gerda was far happier in her new school, as there were other Jewish refugee girls there and she described her time as 'heavenly!'

Apparently it was a non-denominational school founded in 1934 by German 'emigre' Dr Hilde Lyon and Bertha Bracey, a 'Quaker activist' who provided an education for mainly female Jewish refugees from Nazi Europe. Gerda's favourite teachers were Music teacher Dr Louise Leven, Dr Emmy Wolff, German language and Dr Lion Head teacher. She later joined her guarantor Muriel Chadwick at the age of seventeen when Mrs Chadwick had moved to Stratford Upon Avon in 1944.

At the beginning of 1945 Gerda left to go to work on farms in Worcestershire and Surrey, in preparation for life in Palestine on a Kibbutz, but sadly she felt no real vocation for life in Israel and so she moved to London to become an office worker. In 1949, after she married Adolf Mayer from Vienna, who was also a Kindertransport child and Gerda became naturalised as a British Citizen.

In her thirties Gerda read for a degree in Bedford, College University of London, and in 1963 she graduated with a BA in English, German, and History of Art. Gerda wrote her first poem in German at eight years old and then later in English and she became a great poet and author.

I once saw a you tube clip with Gerda Mayer talking about her life, but she seldom talked about her parents because she was greatly effected by their sad demise in the concentration camps.

Gerda Mayer died on 15 July 2021.

From 'Heartache of Grass'
Poem 'Dinosaur Footprints Unearthed In Swanage'
By Gerda Mayer.

Dinosaur Footprints Unearthed In Swanage
Banana- or Marmite sandwiches by the sea
And Charles, and William in soppy grey-felt hats
We tried our wet footprints out on the sand
And Nanny kindly called me Flat footgee

Commendable Swanage. remarked in soft pastel shades
Under light blue or Sailcloth skies you had pearly shells
And fresh air, and stones to climb over- and nursery decorum
Later there was a war, and the sea was fenced off.

Once dinosaurs stamped thereabouts pinpricked packed up
Left antediluvian messages a sort of memento mori
By the way of their footprints. Ours are swept away
And my English days are March-coloured sea-bourne wraiths.

From 'Heartache of Grass'
Poem Mrs K's Letter
by Gerda Mayer

<u>Mrs K's Letter</u>
Dear Sirs I want to disinter
My deceased parents him and her
Could you locate them. Somehow I
Am not quite certain where they lie
But shaken free of earth they'll be
Perfectly good – restored to me.
I long for that,
Please go and look
Into your cemetery book
And having found them send me word
Without delay,
Care of this ward.
I hope to leave here and renew
My life and them.
My thanks to you.

Chapter 18
Peter Walder.

BY PAUL WALDER 2023
From Santiago, Chile.

Trevor Chadwick's first trip from Prague to London was during the first week of January 1939. Trevor had arrived in Prague a few days earlier and after a few brief meetings and interviews, he flew back to England with three children. One of them was my father, Peter Walder and I remember my father saying.
" I remember those years in England, that was the best part of my life."

This moment was present throughout my childhood. It is the detachment of my father from his parents when he was only eight years old. In January 1939, my grandparents handed over their youngest son to an unknown British professor to save him from Nazi persecution. This moment, recounted many times during my childhood, not only haunted me all my life but was also at the core of the constitution of my father's identity and possibly mine too. My grandparents, 'meine grosseltern', arrived at Prague by the end of 1938, fleeing Nazi persecution after the occupation of the Moravia Silesia region, a place in which they had lived since 1935, after moving away from Vienna.

This is the context in which I write Peter's story. There are several sources for this story. The main one, and perhaps the most important, are my memories, which I still hold before an elusive mist. Memory, if we don't capture it, as in a photograph, always tends to vanish and perhaps to be confused with other ancient presences. The other direct sources are later conversations with relatives and old notes. The rest, which is like the canvas, a stage, is made up of the most direct bibliography, press articles, and conversations with descendants of other ancestors.

Peter Walder at Forres School on his bike.   **Forres School, Swanage.**

The drama suffered by the Jews and their children in Germany, Austria and Czechoslovakia was a concern that occupied the newspapers in England in 1938, together with the calls from humanitarian and religious organizations for the search for sponsorship. One such call came to the desk of the Forres School's principal, the Reverend R. M. Chadwick, uncle of the teacher Trevor Chadwick. He was the one who decided to send his nephew and Geoff Phelps, a sports teacher, on a flight to Prague to rescue two children.

Trevor's story, which is in Karen Gershon's book, 'We Came as Children,' is key: "In 1938, I was teaching at my family's elementary school. Rumours reached us of many bereaved children in central Europe and we decided to adopt two according to the Home Office regulations, which required a guarantee of care, and maintenance up to the age of 18, strict personal references of the guarantor, as well as their creditworthiness.

"We travelled with another school teacher to look for the two children. We didn't know where to start, and we had interviews with various people. In a few days we found a couple of small children between eight and ten years old. We had a clear impression of the enormous task. We often saw rooms full of confused refugees and many missing children, most of them Jews." Trevor also recounted in the Gershon book interview the tremendous impression that trip had made on him. "From my arrival I knew that I had to do more. I went to the houses of friends connected with a German childcare movement. They were very busy looking for guarantors and very soon I flew to Prague to look for children to fulfil the requests of the guarantors."

The first two children rescued were Gerard Willi Weigl and my father, Peter Walder, then eight years old. Trevor in the story does not mention them. Yet, years later his Rev William Chadwick also mentioned they brought back to Swanage a young girl called Henrietta, who was sponsored by the parents of Geoff Phelps. "I remember them both very well, especially Gerard Willi, who was one of my friends," William Chadwick recounts in his book about his father.

79

Peter remembered that moment all his life as a key moment, albeit a little blurry, that was also part of my own childhood, detachment and loneliness but also resilience. The lack of an identity, of belonging to a community, to a collective. Life crashed several times but also restarted. Peter always carried a bit of a tragic feeling as a natural destiny, but he also always had the natural strength to continue on his feet. 'One after another,'he used to tell me sometimes when things went wrong.

"There was a school in Dorset that decided to rescue two Jewish children from Central Europe. There was a mission in Prague with one of the teachers from the school to select those two children. My father knew about them and I was one of the children. They put me on a plane on a flight to England where I was throughout the war," Peter recounted in an interview we did with him in 1995.

Another Kinder child Henrietta Wolf-Ferrari aged 14, travelled with Peter and Willi who born in Czechoslovakia, a third passenger who was not included in the plans but who travelled at the impulse and strength of her mother.

Guy Phelps, Geoff's son, recounted that episode many decades later. "Mimi, her mother, had heard about the journey of these young English teachers. She tracked them down and managed to meet them at a restaurant and persuade them to include her daughter, my mother, Henrietta." On January 18th, 1939, she was travelling with Trevor Chadwick, Geoff Phelps and the two children.

Henrietta lived in Geoff's parents' house and did not have a happy life, suffering from the evil effects of the war, especially being a woman and not having a strong grasp of the English language. Henrietta was 4 when she arrived in England and when she turned 16, she would have been seen as a German alien and would have struggled if she had been interrogated with language difficulties.

One day she stopped receiving letters from her mother and her uncles which made her feel vulnerable causing her to worry, as she knew Mimi had been deported in 1943, to the 'Theresienstadt' Concentration Camp and feared they had been killed. She married (or had to) Geoff, her guardian, who was 25 years older than Henrietta. This was a decision that was a step into amplified unhappiness that was passed down for at least a generation. Guy doesn't want to remember much of his childhood; he grew up struck by the echoes and aftershocks of war.

Henrietta separated from Geoff and was unable to remedy her ill-fated life. Guy, a student at the Forres School in Swanage, witnessed the cruel spectre of war in1956, during a walk on the beach. A stray bomb went off and killed six of his teammates, a moment that haunts him to this day. Years later Geoff died of cancer and Henrietta in 1973 in loneliness and pain. His life, emphasized by his son Guy, as being very sad.

That was not the case of Peter, as he was one of the few lucky children who was able to meet his parents years later after the end of the war. Studies carried out later established that out of the ten thousand children who were rescued from Austria and Germany, the Kindertransport operation had more than 600 children from Prague. Yet only a very small percentage were able to see their parents again and this was also a minimal percentage of the total number of children rescued. Of the six million Jews murdered in concentration camps and other killing centres, more than one million were children.

My Aunt Lilly, a sister four years older than my father Peter, also had memories of those days: "When we sent him to England, no one could escape any more. We had no choice. We had tried to go to Australia but there were no visas. We were open to any possibility." Lilly remembered that moment with a special sadness, perhaps because she also sensed the despair of her parents. She also remembered a British man who was undoubtedly Nicholas Winton. "It was the same person who called my father and told him that a group of teachers had come from England to rescue some children. Trevor Chadwick later told 'Mein Opa Leo:' meaning "His son will go."

Trevor Chadwick returned to England in June 1939, and was called up to enlist in the Navy once the war began in September. The famous image of him with the children in Swanage is from those few months, perhaps towards the beginning of autumn according to their clothing.

The photo also clearly reveals his outgoing and fun personality, very cheerful with a bell in one hand and a newspaper in the other, a particularly warm atmosphere reflected in the smiling faces of the children. If the photo was taken in August or September 1939, Peter had only been in Swanage for six months but he looked happy and composed, with Willi Gerald standing by his side and both, under Trevor as the great protective figure.

When the war began, Swanage Forres School was evacuated and they moved to Penn House in Buckinghamshire, in Amersham. This historic place with its classic mansion, belonging to a relative from Chadwick, with its meadows and fish ponds was a paradise for not only for children, but for everybody. Peter remembered this place all his life with great affection and devotion.

More than the first years in Austria and Czechoslovakia with his family on his father's side, his real childhood was here, in this slightly aristocratic English school. "I remember those years in England and it was possibly the best part of my life. They were fantastic people and I remember them with great affection".

Peter was at Forres School until the end of the war and in August 1945, he travelled by ship to Chile to join his family. The trip was probably from Bristol to Buenos Aires, where he stayed for a couple of weeks at the house of the brother of the director of the Forres School who was the Naval Attaché of the British Embassy in Argentina. Peter then went on to travel by plane to 'Santiago de Chile' where his parents and sisters were waiting to receive Peter and took him to their small home in 'Port of Valparaiso.'

The day Peter arrived he couldn't hide his astonishment as the change from the aristocratic atmosphere of Penn House in Buckinghamshire to the austere dwelling on a hill in the Chilean port and which left an impact on him. When he entered the room, he turned to Leo and asked him "Where is the piano?"

His father told him, in his usual calm way,"I'm sorry my boy but we don't have a piano at home". A few years later, and in view of his business consolidation, he gave Peter a piano as a gift, Peter was over the moon. Peter said "My grandfather was a very educated man and spoke English quite well, although with a tremendous German accent," Peter claimed with a bit of sarcasm."Not so with Edith, my grandmother, who in 1945, spoke no English and very little Spanish."

The first letters Peter sent to his parents from England began in Czech, according to my grandmother Edith's account. Weeks later in a mix of German and Czech, a little later a mix of German and English and then all in English. From the first weeks in the boarding school every Sunday and after attending church all the children wrote to their parents. Peter totally forgot his Czech and almost all of his German so that correspondence with his parents could not be in any language other than English. On the other side of the Atlantic, Leo was in charge of writing and translating into English and reading and translating into German.

History has raised Nicholas Winton as the "English Schindler", according to the English popular press. His 'Humanitarian work.' helped save hundreds of children, but it is also that of Doreen Warriner and Trevor Chadwick, known as the "Scarlet Pimpernel" in Czechoslovakia and now the Swanage Schindler. Winton deserves all the praise he has received, in documentaries, newspaper articles, books and the statue erected in Prague's Wilson Station. With the passage of time and the effort of the Swanage community, documents and testimonies have been provided that magnify Trevor Chadwick. Winton himself said that Chadwick was the real hero.

In a dramatic letter sent to 'The Guardian' years ago by Guy Phelps, the son of Henrietta and Geoff, he vindicates the figure of the Forres School teacher. "It was Chadwick who was stationed in Prague and had to select the children (the British guarantors who paid £50 for the privilege of having girls from seven to ten years old and, if possible, blondes) and organized their journey, initially in a plane, then by train. It was Trevor Chadwick, who on one occasion when the Home Office made no effort to provide the necessary documents in the limited time frame, was forced to find someone forging the documents so that the children could get out. Trevor Chadwick even managed to save some adults, smuggled in as "leaders."

It is necessary to imagine the context of these activities. Nazi-occupied Czechoslovakia and Trevor acting in a grey area, in outright illegality under the rule of the SS and Gestapo. An activity that put his life at risk. "You can imagine the risks to himself. He remained in Prague from January to the end of June 1939, when he realized that the Gestapo followed him. That's why he had to leave in a hurry."

"Unfortunately, Chadwick was not the heroic type. He was the black sheep of a conservative Christian family, who had a life and a career full of obstacles and empty spaces. At one point he joined the RAF (Royal Air Force), where he was court-martialled, and later promoted. It's sad that he and Doreen Warriner have been forgotten. I certainly owe my life to Chadwick. He was persuaded to bring my 14-year-old mother with him when he first returned from Prague bringing two children on behalf of the school in Swanage where she taught," Guy wrote.

This text, written by Guy Phelps, speaks for him and also for me and my sisters. I owe him, and we owe him our lives when in that selfless and heroic act he flew from Prague to London with Peter and the other two children.

Peter Gardening   **Peter climbing a tree**

Peter as a young boy
With his Dog.

Peter as a young man
With his dog.

Peter with his grandmother

Peter's family

Peter as a young man in Buenos Aires in Chile.

Guy Phelps, son of Geoff Phelps who went to Prague with Trevor Chadwick, said "As my mother Henrietta Phelps, told it to me, the school had decided, presumably at Trevor instigation, to sponsor two boys to come to England and go to the school. Trevor and my father, Geoffrey, therefore flew to Prague to find two boys. While there they were accosted in a fish restaurant by Henrietta's Grandmother Maria Wolf-Ferrari, who somehow persuaded them also to take my mother. Geoff evidently agreed that his family would sponsor my mother which is what happened and mother lived with the Phelps family while going to boarding school.

When she left aged 18, Geoff thought it would be a good idea they were married. There is no other way in which my mother could have met my father so I cannot believe it is incorrect in any way. I never heard any mention of Gerda Mayer or any other girl on board, let alone two (Gerda referred to a friend who accompanied her which was Hannah Stern).

I think the answer to this conundrum is that Trevor made a subsequent solo trip to Prague and rescued the two girls. The fact that Gerda never mentions my father makes this seem more likely. Both trips presumably preceded Trevor's involvement in the Kindertransport itself which he saw as a more effective way of helping.

I am afraid that once a story has become established it is very difficult to correct almost every article suggests that it was Gerda and not my mother who was the third child rescued by Chadwick (my fathers role is always omitted entirely). According to Chadwick own account (in Karen Gershon's book We came as Children;) it was late in 1938 that Chadwick and my father were sent by the school to Prague to find two boys to be sponsored and were persuaded to take my mother, as described in my previous email.

My mother was only accepted because the Phelps family agreed to sponsor her and indeed looked after her until she was 18, when she married Geoff. Meanwhile, in his diary, Gerda's father wrote that "On 14 March,1939, my Gerda flew by plane to England. Mr Chadwick, who took 20 children along with him, is taking my Gerda to his family; Hitler marched into Prague the next day."

However the fiction is now established and I am tired of trying to correct the story. My poor mother, who had a pretty miserable life - her mother died in Theresienstadt and she herself died aged 49 when her doctor missed symptoms of breast cancer - has now been written out of history. So be it. **'Thanks.'**

One final thought. The best information I have come across about Trevor Chadwick is a long article in the Observer Review of 18 July 1988, written by Elizabeth Cooper and entitled 'The Pimpernel of Prague'. It is quite a detailed account of his life I expect you are aware of this already but if not it should be possible to access it in the Guardian Archive."

The author says, "Only a few people like Sir Nicholas Winton were honoured for their bravery and work with the Kindertransport, saving Jewish Children and other children that didn't fit in with the Aryan Race, from the hands of the Nazi regime. Whilst there were many people who didn't get credit for their heroism for their part in the Kindertransport like Geoffrey Phelps, Trevor Chadwick, Doreen Warriner, Florence Nankivell, Irma Zanker and so many more, who really do deserve to get recognition for their part saving 10,000 children from the gas chamber through the Kindertransport project.

We also have to remember that behind each story there is a back drop of pain, suffering,brokenness, abuse, and yet triumph and the promise of a better life, but I will leave this to the readers imagination to fill in the gaps.

Chapter 19
Letters from Jewish parents
to their Kindertransport children.
'My beloved Children.'
(Translation of the last letter by Irene Csany 1894-1944.)

I'm saying farewell. The pain from being so far from you is unbearable but know that I'm with you in spirit. Love each other and don't forget me. Mrs Fold will see that this note gets to you. She has been a great comfort to me through all this: She is a good soul.

You can rely on my lawyer, Dr Bella Uretty. He handles all my affairs.
Dearest Charles you will be able to claim some money at the orphans court.
Gaby, my darling, my Clothes and furs, if any survive, will be yours.
Charles will know what to do.

My little Charles, the last thing that brought me happiness was the postcard you sent me through Louis's friend. Sell up and go abroad. A million kisses, my dearest ones and embraces,

Your sad, loving mother.

Winton / Chadwick
Kindertransport Child
John Fieldsend.

Page 178 'A Wondering Jew' by John Fieldsend.

Farewell letter to John Fieldsend and his brother from their parents, Curt and Trudy Feige before, their interment to Auschwitz.

From John's Mother

Dear Boys when you receive this letter the war will be over because our friendly messenger won't be able to send it earlier. We want to say 'farewell' to you who were our dearest possessions in the world, and only for a short time were we able to keep you.

Fate has not left us for months now. In Jan.1942 the Weilers were taken, we still don't know where to and whether they are still alive. In June Grandmother Betty, in September Aunt Marion, Uncle Willi and Pauli, in Oct. your Steiner grandparents, in Nov. Your 90 year old Great Grandmother and the Berman's. In Dec. it will be our turn and that time has therefore come for us to turn to you again and to ask you to become good men and to think of the years that we were happy together. We are going into the unknown; not a word is to be heard from those already taken.

Thank the Cumpsty's who have kept you from a similar fate. You took of course a piece of your parent's hearts with you when we decided to give you away. Give our thanks and gratitude to all who are good to you.

From John's Father

Your dear mother has told you about the hard fate of all our loved ones. We too will not be spared and will go bravely into the unknown with the hope that we shall yet see you again when God wills. Don't forget us, and be good.
I too thank all good people who have accepted you so nobly.

The Author says,"As you can see it was very painful for parents of Kindertransport children to give their children up, and send them to Britain with the knowledge of what was to be their own fate. What upset them so much was the fact they would never see their children again. However not all children wanted to leave Germany and come to England, in fact many felt like it was an 'exodus' being sent away from their family, friends and country."

Chapter 20
Poem, 'The Children's Exodus'
From 'We Came As Children' page 171

It was an ordinary train
Travelling across Germany
Which gathered and took us away
Those who saw it may have thought
That it was a holiday
Not being exiled being taught
To hate what we loved in vain
brought us lasting injury

Our parent's let us go
Knowing that who stayed must die.
But kept the truth from us although
They gave us to reality
Did they consider what they many
To become orphaned and not know
To be emotionally freed
When our childhood seeds were spent

But each child was one refugee
We unlike the Egyptian salves
Carrying Six million lives
That was Jewish history
But each child was one refugee
We unlike the Egyptian slaves
Were exiled Individually
And each in desolation has
Created his own wilderness

This race hatred was personal
We were condemned what we were
No one escaped the ritual
From which we rose Inferior
The blood guilt entered every home
Till daily life was a progrom
We who were are not the same
As those who have no wreck to share
Home is were some know who you are
The rescue was impersonal
It was no ones concern what use

We made of the years given us
One should not ask of children who
Find their survival natural
Gratitude for being where
Ten thousand others have come too

At Dovercourt the winter sea
Was like God's mercy vast and wild
A fever to a land - locked child
It seemed fire and cloud to me
The worlds blood and my blood were cold
The exiled Jew in me was old
and thought's of death appalled me less
Than knowledge of my loneliness

My mother sold my bed and chair
While expected to return
Yet she had kept me close to her
Till I saw our temple burn
It was not for sake but for mine
She knew that I was unripe fruit
And that exile was a blight
Against which one prepared in vain

People at Dovercourt were gay
As if they thought we could forget
Our homes in alien play
As if we were not German Jews
But mealtimes were a market place
When sudden visitor's could choose
Although we weren't orphaned yet
A son or daughter by their face

My childhood smoulders in the name
Of the town of which was my home
All we were became no more
Than answers on each questionnaire
At Dovercourt we were taught that
Our share of the Jewish fate
Had not been left behind but was the refugee life facing us .

Chapter 21
Other Kindertransport Children in Swanage

Other children in Swanage who were Kindertransport Children Jewish refugees were: -

1.Kurt Eisenbach who became Kurt Ellington spoken about in Alfred Batzdorf's account of life in Swanage.

2.Gerald Willi Weigl

In the book **'Swanage Wartime Childhood' by Stewart Borret**t we read in Richard Hill - Browns account of his 'wartime childhood in Swanage ' pages 50-51 :-

" My mother did work briefly at the Grammar school as a dinner lady, but her war was mostly spent in looking after us and a whole succession of lodgers. My very earliest memory is of standing in our front room surrounded by big chair arms and adult knees, and hearing voices laughing, not unkindly at me. Later I learned these were German and Austrian Jewish refugees and they were teaching me to say "Guten Morgen". Our warm-hearted Yorkshire mother had met one Berlin couple by chance and invited them to call whenever they were free. (Could this have been Mr and Mrs Batzdorf ?) Early in 1939 other refugees arrived and 222 High Street Swanage became for a while their informal 'clubhouse'. A six year old, Ulla stayed with us rather than at her parent's place of work. When war began they all had to leave Swanage for the Midlands. The first couple, who were Ulla's uncle and aunt returned to Swanage after the war and remained among my parent's best friends."

Page 63 Valerie Shepherd
In the early part of the war I went from school to school in different parts of England and ended up at A' Beckets, a girls boarding school at Littleton Panell Wiltshire. It was at this school that I met Inge an Austrian Jewish refugee, who had come over from Vienna, on Kindertransport in 1938.

Inge's father had been a civil engineer on the team that re-enforced concrete in Vienna. He was interned as an enemy alien and therefore she couldn't return to be with him in the school holidays, so she went to stay with a friend in Kent.
As I was the only child I asked Inge if she would like to come to stay at our house, so some holidays she's come to us and some to Sally Minet's house in Kent. In the end Inge came to stay permanently and became part of the family. Her father was in full agreement with the arrangement.

Page 64 'Swanage wartime childhood' by Stewart Borrett.

My mother and I lived with my grandmother in a small village called Worton but my mother was keen to move and get her own house. Mother had connections with Swanage and she had known the town as a child. My Mother, Inge, and I moved to Swanage in late Summer 1941 and went to live in 'Almondbury' in Kings Road West. Inge and I were 12 years old at the time.

Later on we moved down the road to Thorvaton which backed onto the railway. This house had three rooms and a box room stuffed with trunks. On the ground floor there was the usual dining room with a blue planted Morrison shelter, (an iron frame that fitted under the table which protected the people inside from falling debris) a sitting room and a kitchen at the back. Inge and I shared a bedroom.

Page 68

In 1945 Inge reached the age of 16, a Policeman appeared at the door of our house one day and said." I believe you have an enemy alien here," We were extremely astonished. Inge had never considered herself as an enemy alien but as she continued to have Austrian nationality this was certainly the case; the Policeman was very nice about it. He said "Enemy aliens are not allowed to live within 10 miles of the coast, however if you register every month at the police station at the cost of one shilling that would be in order."

Inge's father was interned as an enemy alien for quote some time. Enemy aliens were refugees and mostly Jewish from the European countries overrun with Nazis. The Government may think they are German spies planted amongst them, so they were separated into three groups. The first group were considered quite safe and were allowed to stay in their own homes and take jobs.

The third group were considered dangerous and interned immediately and one or two cases shipped to Australia. The middle group were unsure and interned usually for a short time only, but later like Inge's father given the opportunity to leave the internment camp and join the Royal Pioneer Corps. Internment didn't apply to young people under the age of 16 and under normal circumstances no enemy aliens could live within 10 miles of the coast. (The Royal Pioneer Corps,dug trenches one day and filled them the next)

Page 69

Inge went to the Secretarial College, Knyveton Road, Bournemouth (Boscombe). Then went back to her father and stepmother in London.

Valerie and Inge after the war   **Virgil and Friedl Berger**
                                        Austrian Jews On Swanage beach 1939

Taken from 'Swanage Wartime Childhood' by Stewart Borrett

WITH THANKS:-

Firstly I would like to thank the **'Great I Am,'** King of the Universe for revealing Trevor Chadwick and Alfred Batzdorf to me through Purbeck Coast Radio Swanage, Josephine Jackson who gives talks about Kindertransport and Edith Powney the organiser of Holocaust Memorial in Wimborne, Dorset.

Thank you Mick and Rosemary, Radio Presenters of Purbeck Coast Radio Swanage for introducing the station one Sunday afternoon at Durleston. You told me that I should join and now the rest is history. 'It was simply meant to be.' God had a plan and purpose that through 'Purbeck Coast Radio' to find Trevor and Alfred.

 I would also like to thank :-
Edith Powney,Wimborne Holocaust Memorial Organiser and friend.
Josephine Jackson, Kindertransport expert and Speaker.
John Corben, Chairman Trevor Chadwick Trust.
Paul Walder, Son of Peter Walder.
Guy Phelps. Son of Geoff and Henrietta Phelps.
Edmund Nankivell. Son of Florence Nankivell.
Craig Saul. Son of Gary Saul.
For sharing their stories concerning Kindertransport.
I thank the authors of the books I found with so much information about Swanage and Kindertransport connection.

I thank Purbeck Coast Radio for being the vehicle to discover Trevor Chadwick by hosting Edith and Josephine on 'Lunchtime with Elaine', as when I googled Holocaust and Swanage it came up with 'Trevor Chadwick and Kindertransport.'
Thank you to Station Manager Michelle for being supportive of this project.

I would also like to thank and acknowledge the work of 'Trevor Chadwick Trust' for raising money for the statue to be sculpted by Moira Purver.

I would like to thank Mora Purver for the statute of 'Trevor and the children,' it is truly a 'master piece' and I know it will have taken a lot of hard work, love, sweat and tears. God had the right person for the job.

I would like to thank Nick Winton and Samuel Chadwick for coming to Swanage and unveiling the Sculpture of 'Swanage Schindler' and 'Hero' Trevor Chadwick.

I would like to thank Cathy Brocklehurst and Edith Powney, for their advice and helping me edit my book.

You can find Alfred's Video with Holocaust Memorial Oral History
https://collections.ushmm.org/search/catalog/irn509536